Soaring In Sonship Series

ROOTED IN SONSHIP

Fruitful & Flourishing In Abiding

NICHOLAS BARTA
Foreword by Lisa Max

CONTENTS

Endorsements — v
Foreword — xiii
Acknowledgments — xvii
Introduction — xix

1. Living In Life-Union with Jesus — 1
   The Adventure of a Lifetime
2. The Gentle Heart Gardener — 15
   The Voice of The Good Shepherd
3. A Renewed Mind — 29
   Thinking Through Your Heart
4. Abiding Rest — 45
   The Sweet Fruit of Rest
5. The Parable of Parables — 55
   The Parable Of The Sower
6. The Fear Of The LORD — 69
   What's Missing In The Church?
7. Obedient Love — 83
   Trust In Him
8. A Friend Of God — 99
   Infinite Access And Fullness
9. Abiding Prayer — 109
   Hearts Beating As One
10. Trials Into Triumphs — 125
    Chosen And Set Apart
11. Victorious Sonship — 139
    Stones Of Remembrance
12. Be Fruitful And Multiply — 151
    Fruitfulness In All Seasons

Epilogue — 167

About the Author — 169
Also by Nicholas Barta — 171
Resources — 175
Notes — 177

Rooted in Sonship: Fruitful and Flourishing In Abiding
Soaring In Sonship Series - Book 2

Copyright © 2024 by Nicholas Barta

All rights reserved. This book or any portion thereof may not be reproduced or used in any manner whatsoever without the express written permission of the author except for the use of brief quotations in a book review. To request permissions, contact Nicholas Barta @ info@soaringsonsanddaughters.com. For more information, please visit:

Soaring Sons and Daughters[1]
9975 Wadsworth Pkwy., K-2 #267
Westminster, CO 80021

Unless otherwise noted, all scripture is taken from the New King James Version®. Copyright ©1982 by Thomas Nelson. Used by permission. All rights reserved.

Foreword by Lisa Max, Let The Children Fly
Editor, Anne Thompson, Ebookannie Design
Cover Design, Alice Briggs, Kingdom Covers
Interior Design, Anne Thompson, Ebookannie Design

Rooted in Sonship: Fruitful and Flourishing In Abiding /
Nicholas Barta. ---- 1st ed.

ISBN Paperback: 979-8-9862337-2-7

For Worldwide Distribution. Printed in the United States of America
1 2 3 4 5 6 7 8 9 10

ENDORSEMENTS

God is really BIG! Yet I often find people gravely underestimate His bigness, His goodness, His grace and mercy, and infinite love. More than anyone I have yet met, Nicholas and Michelle spend their lives plumbing the depths of God's big Father's heart. Every aspect of their lives and ministry reflects loving sonship to their magnificent, all-embracing, ever-present heavenly Father. And then they draw others into that ever-expanding revelation. Their love of the Father and then to others is magnetic and contagious. With great joy, I recommend them to you and their ministry at Abba's Table!

Tracy Evans
iReach Africa
Mozambique, Africa

Rooted in Sonship will take you into what it looks like to live a life *Fruitful and Flourishing In Abiding*. Your desire for a life-union with Jesus will either be sparked or renewed as you travel with Nicholas on this adventure of a lifetime that he so passionately unfolds within the pages of this book before you. Get lost in your own adventure with the One who longs to also abide with you!

Gwen Young
BridgeWay Church
Denver, CO

Are you feeling spiritually parched and longing for a refreshing sip of His Living Water? Nicholas eloquently guides you beyond your own struggles to intimately connect with the heart and encouragement of Jesus. Embracing your identity as a beloved child of God inspires you to be rooted in His boundless love with renewed confidence, fueling a passion to share that love with a hurting world—for His glory.

Nicholas reminds us of the importance of abiding, waiting, listening, and obediently following the Holy Spirit's guidance without presumption. Trusting that leading promises abundant fruitfulness, equipping you to fulfill your destiny as a representative of His Kingdom.

Camille Curry
Bus Stop Ministries
Denver, CO

Rooted In Sonship helps establish the firm foundations of walking and abiding in life union with Abba Father, the Son, and the Holy Spirit and ignites a deep hunger for intimacy. The imagery of intimate fellowship with Christ in this book helps to draw the reader into an encounter and to activate the truth of God's Word in our lives. Nicholas effectively communicates significant and profound spiritual principles that help to impart grace and understanding to us to overcome every attack and lie of the enemy by dismantling demonic strongholds to pave the way to walk in health and wholeness as children of God.

This book challenges every believer to take a step back and realize that signs and wonders are released as we are anchored in sonship and identity in Christ. If the church today grasps this revelation of abiding and aims to cultivate this daily, then we will truly see revival sweep and a move of God take place in churches, families, homes, neighborhoods and cities around the world! The church truly needs this book now more than ever! We strongly recommend this book as a key to truly receiving a revelation of sonship and becoming more deeply rooted and grounded in the perfect love of Jesus.

Neil and Brittany Sanderlin
Radiant House International
Castle Rock, CO

I dedicate this book to my closest best friend and companion, the Holy Spirit. The nearness and intimacy I've experienced through fellowship with the Holy Spirit are beyond the greatest treasure in my life. There are not enough words to describe the joy, the beautiful passion, and the deep fulfillment of the love of living in close intimacy with the Lord. I am forever grateful to God for extending this friendship and intimacy to each of us. Thank You, Holy Spirit, for your presence, Your love, and Your anointing to write this work for the glory of King Jesus! I love you, Abba Father, Jesus Christ, and Holy Spirit!

I also dedicate this work to my beautiful family for all the sacrifices you've made to bless Daddy to write and work on this message. Thank you to my beautiful children for your love, prayers, support, and prophetic insight sown into the writing of this book. I honor you, Michelley, my beautiful beloved wife and best friend for always standing by my side and supporting me through thick and thin to press forward and onwards to championing the message of Sonship. You've inspired, supported, strengthened, and encouraged me to continue moving forward into the upward call of God in Christ Jesus, and I am forever grateful for you. Together as one in the Lord, we share the great joy of releasing this message of Sonship and abiding oneness to touch and transform the hearts of all those who read it and encounter Him. To God be all the glory!

"So you must remain in life-union with me, for I remain in life-union with you. For as a branch severed from the vine will not bear fruit, so your life will be fruitless unless you live your life intimately joined to mine."

—John 15:4 TPT

FOREWORD

We can easily imagine the difference between a child born into an orphanage and a child brought home from the hospital, adored by an attentive mother and father. The one in the orphanage grows up learning how to depend upon themselves for everything. Their primary function is to look out for their survival and safety and meet their basic needs. Children raised in the safety of a loving home with a mom and dad can thrive and explore life because their parents manage their basic needs and create a culture of love, acceptance, and empowerment. We don't always transfer this image into the Church as it relates to our relationship with our heavenly Father. Spiritual orphans can spend their entire lifetime using all of their time, energy, and resources to care for their own needs, never learning how to receive God as their Father. A good son or daughter is still just a spiritual orphan without a father. To function as true sons and daughters, one must have a deeper revelation of their Father's role and involvement in their life.

Some people believe that God, the Father, controls everything; therefore, they don't need to do much except accept life as it comes actively. Others strive and try hard to be good enough and please Him on their own. Could God's original design for His children be that there is a mutual exchange, and both have a purpose and role in having a healthy connec-

Foreword

tion? John 15:5 explains this further: "I am the vine; you are the branches. If a man remains in me and I in him, he will bear much fruit; apart from me, you can do nothing." The secret to a fruitful life is understanding our responsibility to remain in Him and the revelation of Him in us, the definition of Sonship.

I met Nicholas after first meeting the wrong guy. We laugh about the story every time we recall it, but truthfully, it isn't just a funny memory; it has become a part of Nicholas' journey.

Let me explain.

We were visiting our home church in Denver when God gave me a powerful and clear word for Nicholas. The problem was I hadn't met him yet and didn't share it with him when the service ended, as we were both ministering elsewhere. Months later, the words still burned in my heart, but I didn't know who he was to share them. We found ourselves on another trip, and I saw a man worshiping up front who, from behind, looked like the guy God gave me a word for months ago. I eagerly went up to him and released the prophetic word. The look on his face told me he did not receive it, and it was inaccurate for him. Later that day, a mutual friend who overheard me give the word asked me about it, and I told him the story. He said, "I think you meant Nicholas, as the two look so familiar, many mistake them for each other." Shortly after I ran into the real Nicholas, I gave him the word God had given me months earlier that was still burning in my heart. The gist of the word was that his current challenging and crushing circumstances were training grounds. Despite his young natural age, I told him God was raising him up to the level of maturity of a senior leader. The word encouraged him to yield to the process, watch, and see what God would do through his obedience.

Sure enough, in a short time, Nicholas and his wife, Michelle, would launch and plant Abba's Table church, where he functions as senior pastor. Few people embody the message of Sonship as a lifestyle as Nicholas does. He has a single-minded focus on how he cares for his family, parents, and children and leads God's people - through the lens of how a son would respond. I have watched Nicholas go through the agonizing process of willfully choosing to die to himself and crucify the

Foreword

places where self reigns to find oneness with Jesus. This isn't a journey anyone can do for you or hand to you; it is yielding to God's holy invitation. Nicholas has accepted this invitation as his life's work.

While he is an incredible Jesus-hearted leader, his strength is in his Sonship. When leaders operate as sons and daughters first, the fruit is healthy. When leaders function out of leadership first, they produce spiritual orphans. Only true sons and daughters can produce sons and daughters in God's Kingdom.

Many years ago, long before God birthed our ministry, *Let the Children Fly*, our church hosted a large regional conference with many big-name speakers. My spiritual father, John, came to me and said, "Lisa, it's time!" It was time for me to step out and pray for people. I had done all the training, and it was time to apply it in faith and step out. I argued I wasn't ready and feared nothing would happen if I prayed for people. I was wracked with insecurity and doubt.

Yet John saw something in me I didn't. I knew I would not win the argument and sheepishly submitted to his invitation. He assured me with the words, "Lisa, my hand is on your back." I assumed that meant he would sit on the side of the stage where this gentle giant could often be found on assignment, praying over the activity in the room.

I took a deep breath and rationalized that the people up front would want the main leaders to pray for them and would be disappointed if I came to them, so I talked myself into praying for the people in the aisles, assuming they probably would be happy with someone praying for them since they couldn't make it to the front. I lifted my hesitant hand to the first person, and boom, without notice, they fell to the ground and were encountering God profoundly. The second person had the same response. The third, fourth, and fifth people encountered God before I could finish my prayer. By the twelfth person, I was perplexed by what was happening until I turned around and saw John standing behind me with his hand over my back. I wept. Was it his anointing or mine? It didn't matter. We were doing this together as one.

As I have shared that testimony, people cry with longing over the years. They want that kind of hand-on-my-back covering. They want someone

Foreword

who sees something in them and calls it out. They want someone to believe in them and champion them. Despite a million reasons why they aren't qualified, they want a spot at the table. We have that with Jesus Christ. He doesn't just live in us; we live in Him. That is what *Rooted In Sonship* is all about. Allow Nicholas to unpack your journey of discovering just how real, tangible, and personal Jesus is in your life, to lead you to your spot at His table, and to show you how to live together as one truly. Jesus is coming back for a Bride, not an orphan. I believe we are in the season where the garment of His Bride is being fitted properly upon her. The garment is Sonship!

Lisa Max, Director of *Let The Children Fly*, is a ministry that empowers parents to partner with the Holy Spirit in their parenting. Lisa has developed over the years from mothering mothers into mothering ministries. With a strong apostolic call and heart, she longs to see parents and leaders walking as healthy, deeply connected Sons and Daughters so that they can raise a generation that is seen, heard, and valued. Lisa is the author of *JOURNEY: Partnering with Holy Spirit in Your Parenting*, *HEART SPLINTERS: Resolving Childhood Owies in Childhood*, and *HURT IN THE CHURCH: Healing What Was Stolen*. She can be found at home enjoying her family, hosting monthly mentorship groups for parents, and transforming communities by creating healthy families.

Lisa Max
Director of *Let The Children Fly*,
Author, Speaker, Coach, Mentor, Podcaster

ACKNOWLEDGMENTS

I want to thank the Lord for His unending, enduring love that continues to fuel my life with adventure and passion to write and share the messages He leads me to share. I want to thank my publishing team, including Anne Thompson, Alice Briggs, and the SelfPublishing.com team. Anne, I'm so grateful for your attention to detail, anointing as a passionate lover of Jesus, and tender care to protect my author's voice and the purity of this message. Thank you, Alice, for your patience in working on all the small details to get the cover design perfect to powerfully communicate this message. Thank you, Lisa, for your love and influence in my life and my family's lives. We are so grateful for you and for how you are a champion for the Lord as you continue fighting to take the mountain of family for God's glory. I also want to thank the spiritual mothers and fathers in my life who have mentored me and sown into this work and the message of sonship. This would not have been possible without their involvement and influence in my life, and I am deeply thankful for all they have sown in the garden of my life to develop these deep roots of Sonship in the Lord. Of these, I want to especially honor and thank Mama Tracy Evans for living the message of Sonship and abiding in Jesus more powerfully and profoundly than I ever imagined. Mama Tracy, your life is a living epistle of the Lord, and you have deeply and forever impacted our lives by living your laid-down life for the Lord Jesus. Thank you for your authenticity, love, prayers, and tremendous wisdom, which you've sown into us over the years. We forever treasure you in our lives and in the lives of our beautiful children. May we steward these Kingdom seeds sown into us and produce fruit from intimacy that will remain through the tides of time for the glory of the beloved Son of God, Jesus Christ, our True Vine!!

INTRODUCTION

Few things in life captivate us in such a way that when we read it, we instantly desire to become deeply changed and transformed from the inside out. When we open the Bible and read the words penned by the Holy Spirit through the hands and hearts whom God selected, thousands of years later, we are still being transformed by God's grace through the power of His holy Word. As we dive into God's Word with humility and hunger of heart, we discover more of who He is and who we are in Him. We learn from the first chapter in the gospel of John, "In the beginning was the Word, and the Word was with God, and the Word was God" (John 1:1). Jesus Christ is the fullness of the expression of the heart of the Father to all of creation. He is the only begotten Son of the Father and is the Word of God that became flesh (John 1:14).

Imagine for a moment from Father God's perspective. In His complete sovereignty, Father God appointed His Son Jesus to be the full expression of His heart, His words, and His love for all of creation (Heb 1:3). God existed before anything in the world was created. In His eternal existence, remaining in three persons as one, God the Father, God the Son, and God the Holy Spirit, God expressed His design and desire for *family* to all of His creation. In the Holy Trinity, we see a perfect relationship of complete unity and oneness, a family expressed for all of creation to experience the

Introduction

unfailing, ever-flowing love between the Father, the Son, and the Holy Spirit as one. The Holy Trinity never intended for the unbreakable bond of intimacy and love to only remain within them.

In His unimaginable glory and heart expression of perfect love, Father God always planned from the beginning to create mankind in His very image and likeness (Gen 1:27) and to not only invite them in, but to fully fuse them together in eternal relational oneness with Him. When Adam and Eve sinned in the garden, God already had the plan to send His only begotten Son, Jesus, to redeem mankind from the curse of sin and separation from Him. Revelation 13:8 teaches us that Jesus, the Lamb of God, was slain before the foundation of the world was made. Jesus paid the way at the whipping post and the cross to save and redeem mankind back into the right relationship with our Triune God. The glorious blood of Jesus Christ, KING of kings and LORD of lords welcomes us back into the original design of family in oneness with God, not only in eternity but also here on earth in this life.

Sons and daughters of God, if you have received Jesus as Lord of your life in your heart, and you have confessed Him as your personal Lord and Savior, His blood has redeemed you, and you have been born again and welcomed back into this glorious oneness with God. In this oneness, there is no separation, distance, or hierarchy. Through Jesus Christ, God has invited all who receive to come into the revelation of endless love in this life and in the life to come. Along with all the sons and daughters across the earth and through the ages, together as born-again believers, we are making up the family of God and will spread the message of the gospel of Jesus Christ to all four corners of the earth. Through Jesus' triumph over sin and death, when He rose from the grave and ascended into heaven, He empowered us to live and reign on the earth as God's beloved and cherished family. We embrace glorious sons and daughters from every beautiful color of skin and from every tribe, nation, and tongue. The times that we are now living in are the great emergence of the revelation of the Father's love and of His heart to engraft His children into oneness with Him as His family for all eternity. How exciting and unimaginably glorious it truly is that we should be called children of God, who get the privilege and blessing to live in oneness as His family upon the earth and for all eternity!

Perhaps there is no better simple revelation of the price that Jesus paid through His death and resurrection than to understand it in these three words: all for LOVE. It was all for love that Jesus humbled Himself, in the form of mankind, leaving His divinity and living His life, demonstrating to us how to live a life anchored in sonship (the spirit of adoption) and oneness with God through abiding continuously in the love of our heavenly Father. In everything that Jesus was and in everything that He did, He did so as the beloved Son of the Father. There was nothing more important to Jesus than to live in constant life-union with His heavenly Father through the power of the Holy Spirit and to commune with Him always in everything He did. When we look at the glorious life of Jesus Christ, we see in Him THE example of living and reigning together with God in this life.

Before Jesus was to be betrayed and handed over to the religious authorities to be crucified, He taught His disciples some of the most important principles and revelations for living in this life. In John chapters 13-17, we read of Jesus' last discourse before He went to the cross. In chapters 15 and 17, we learn about what it truly means to abide in and with the Lord and to live in oneness with Him. God's heart is for every son and daughter to know just how much He loves us and to experience infinite intimacy with Him as we live out our lives for His glory upon the earth. Jesus came to reveal to us the heart of the Father, and to all those who receive Jesus, He has commissioned us to reveal Him to the world. It's not merely enough to preach the gospel and share it with others; we also must show it (1 Cor 4:20). We can show the gospel to others most powerfully by accessing the intimate love of oneness with God that we receive through continually abiding in and with Him. This will diffuse the aroma of Jesus to all the world through our surrendered lives (2 Cor 2:15). This is the oneness, the life union that Jesus spoke of, as recorded in John 15 and 17. It is through our willingness to receive God's love that we will become transformed by His love and then release His love to those around us so that they may experience the love of God that hung on that cross for their

Introduction

salvation and reconciliation back into the loving arms of our heavenly Father.

Son or daughter of God, this is exactly the intent of this book: to awaken, teach, equip, and activate you deeper and more profoundly in the revelation of the love of God through learning how to abide in Him every day and in every season of life. Jesus said in John 15:5, "I am the vine, you *are* the branches. He who abides in Me, and I in him, bears much fruit; for without Me you can do nothing." Our central aim in living as Christians in this life should be to learn to abide in Jesus just as He abides in His Father. We must posture our hearts in such a way that we capture the revelation of oneness with God found in His Word so that we can bring every trace of division, distraction, doubt, separation, and unbelief into submission before the Lordship of Jesus. As a result, His unfailing love will transform us.

God's heart is for every son and daughter of His to learn and live in the fullness of His affection through total access to Him, depending on Him to lead and guide us in the way we should go all throughout our lives (Ps 32:8). As we open our hearts and our minds to press into learning how to abide in the Lord, we will experience the manifestation of oneness with the Father, Son, and Holy Spirit in ever-increasing ways as we live our lives in life-union with God. Jesus is the way, the truth, and the life who leads us on the pathway to eternal life with the Lord. As we hunger to grow, mature, and blossom in living abiding in the true vine, He will teach and impart to us the lifestyle of love that will transform our hearts and minds while increasing our understanding of living at onement with the Lord as His beloved, cherished family. Living at onement gives the Lover of your soul an all-access pass to all of your heart to become transformed by perfect love so that you may represent to the world the true love of Jesus Christ. Through this pure representation of the love of God through the gospel of Jesus will come miracles, signs, and wonders by the Holy Spirit that testify to the risen Son of God.

It's time for us to live and burn with a greater revelation and lifestyle of abiding oneness so that we can preach and show the world through the power of the Holy Spirit, the manifest love of God that saves, heals, delivers, and sets the captives free! To King Jesus be all the glory, honor, and highest praise!! Now, let's dive deep into uncovering more of abiding oneness in living in life-union with Jesus.

> "I do not pray for these alone, but also for those who will believe in Me through their word; that they all may be one, as You, Father, *are* in Me, and I in You; that they also may be one in Us, that the world may believe that You sent Me. And the glory which You gave Me I have given them, that they may be one just as We are one: I in them, and You in Me; that they may be made perfect in one, and that the world may know that You have sent Me, and have loved them as You have loved Me" (John 17:20-23).

1

LIVING IN LIFE-UNION WITH JESUS
THE ADVENTURE OF A LIFETIME

Imagine you were sitting with Jesus outside on a warm autumn day with a cool, refreshing breeze whirling through the air and the warm sunshine glistening on your face. This day, there was no schedule, no timeline, and no expectations from you. It's just you and Jesus. Your personal calendar is wide open, with not a thought in your mind granted to any concerns about what time it is or what will happen next. Your heart, mind, and body feel completely at rest with not a care in the world. There are no thoughts of what you have to do tomorrow or of what you didn't get done yesterday. Your mind is at peace and is not concerned with anything you feel you need to do or to be as you are sitting with Jesus. Suddenly you know everything inside you feels at rest. Everything inside feels like it is in perfect peace. This sensation is overtaking you as you continue to become increasingly amazed at how good it feels to just sit and be with Jesus. You take in a few deep breaths that feel so refreshing and life-giving as you breathe out yesterday and breathe in this fresh new day.

Then, you look over at Jesus to find Him gazing at you with such a joyful delight in His facial expression. You have absolutely no doubts or any question in your mind that Jesus is absolutely thrilled to be with you. You see in His eyes no concern or worry about anything. Somehow, you know in your heart that absolutely nothing else is occupying His thoughts.

Nothing has taken any capacity in His mind about anything else besides *you*. He is enthralled with you, and as you gaze into His eyes, you become overwhelmed with the goodness and pure pleasure shining from His eyes into yours. For a moment, you ponder to yourself, "Is His gaze truly for me? Is His gaze because of me?" Before you can even finish your thought, Jesus speaks with a soft, tender-loving tone in His voice while looking deep into your eyes, "I'm so happy to be here with you."

Your heart floods with great joy and a deep appreciation of Jesus' words over you. Inside you want to respond and say something, yet you can't find any words as you are lost in His ocean eyes of love for you. A moment passes and you realize in your heart that He already knows what you desire to say, but you've already spoken through your heart and gaze back into His eyes. As you look into Jesus' eyes and He continues to look back into yours, He laughs with such great joy. His laughter releases freedom in you as you join in with Him with a playful chuckle. In a joyful disposition, Jesus says, "I love you too!" Your heart explodes with contentment in knowing that He already knew what was in your heart to say.

Jesus now turns His body and faces you with that glorious smile. In great anticipation of wondering what He wants to say, you quickly shuffle and reposition your body to face Him and hear what He has to say. Jesus' pure gaze pierces even deeper into your heart with His perfect love. His holy, scarred hands reach out and gently hold your face as His words flow as a symphony of love into your whole being. "I love you with an everlasting love. My love will never deplete nor ever run out for you, My beloved child." Your emotions are surging as Jesus' words fill new places in your heart and awaken parts of you that haven't experienced His love like this before.

While still holding you, He gives a warm and adventurous invitation to you with a single question, "Will you come away with Me?" As love now fills your whole being with adventure ringing in your heart, you answer expectantly, "Yes Jesus! I will come!!" With great delight filling His face, He holds your face and stares back into your eyes with pure love. It seems like an eternity has passed as you gaze back at Him. Your heart feels a deeper belonging and a greater knowing in your soul about just how much the King of the universe LOVES to be with *YOU*!

Now slowly removing His hands from your face, He takes your hands and stands up as you follow His lead. Jesus embraces you with a huge warm hug as you wrap your arms around Him. After a good long embrace, Jesus takes your hand and asks you, "Are you ready, My sweet child? I have many great things to show you. It's going to be an incredible adventure!" Without even thinking, you respond as a little child would and shouted, "I'm ready! Let's go Jesus!" As you both face out in the warm autumn sun overlooking the beautiful open meadows, blue sky, and stunning mountains, you can feel such excitement in your heart like you've not experienced in years.

Now side by side, Jesus turns His head and says to you, "I'm going to reveal to you the depths of My love that you have not yet known, and you will never be the same! Come, let us journey onward in this incredible adventure!" Taking His hand, you don't look back. You leap forward with great joy and excitement because you know that the great, I Am is leading the way. In leaving everything behind, you know one thing remains.... the rest and peace you experienced sitting next to Jesus. Jesus turns and says one more thing before stepping forward into His invitation. "Only this is required from you, and that is that you abide in Me as I abide in you. Now come away with Me and let Me show you My glorious love." With no hesitation, you grab a hold of His hand, looking into the distance, and together as one, you leap forward with Jesus into the adventure of a lifetime.

Life-Union with Jesus as One

Isn't it incredible when we take time to imagine what God's perfect love is truly like?! When we slow down and simply position our heart in rest to receive His love afresh into our heart, the fruit of receiving becomes immeasurable in our lives. Just a moment in His presence can feel like an eternity when yet only a few minutes or hours have passed. I guess that's why Almighty God holds time in His hands, so that He can bend and twist it any way He pleases to accomplish all He desires in us and through us. To God, a day is as a thousand years and a thousand years is as a day (2 Pet 3:8).

However, in our walk with God in our modern day, it's difficult to find that space of rest and peace in His presence. In a world full of countless distractions, noise, demands and opportunities, it can sometimes seem all too easy to slip out of the quiet place of intimately receiving God's love and fall into a lifestyle of constant noise and busyness. In our fast-paced world, it can feel almost impossible to slow down and find time to read, pray, and be quiet in the presence of the Lord. It can feel almost impossible to drown out all the noise and simply sit and *abide* with Jesus, just as in this vision. However difficult this may seem to fight for this place of abiding with Him, I assure you that no matter what you may have on your plate in life, God is more than capable to show you the way to carve the room and make the space for you to be with Him. For you to *abide* in Him.

This is something that is most important to the heart of God. It is more important than anything we could ever *do* for God, and even more important than anything that we could ever *become* in terms of merit or status in this life for Him. Although we are called to do good works for the Lord that bring glory and honor to Him, this should never come at the cost of our intimacy with Him. Doing good works for the Lord is necessary and needed in this world, but it should never come at the cost of trading our growth in intimacy with God for it. True good works flow from the life of a son or daughter who has learned to abide with the Lover of their soul. For every one of us walking this earth, there is no one who cannot grow more in love with Jesus, and find new ways to abide in Him in the busyness of life. Rather than some kind of expectation that we can never meet, God is giving an invitation that we cannot refuse! He is calling His children, His beloved sons and daughters, to come up higher with Him and to learn what it means to abide in Him as He abides in us. John 15:4 in The Passion Translation says,

> "So you must remain in life-union with me, for I remain in life-union with you. For as a branch severed from the vine will not bear fruit, so your life will be fruitless unless you live your life intimately joined to mine" (John 15:4 TPT).

The invitation is for us to abide in His love and in unison with Him as we walk about this life here on the earth. Our good works for the Lord are never to precede growing intimately in oneness with Him. In all the noise of this life, nothing is more important than learning to be loved by God, and continually growing in receiving His love for you.

God desires for His children to become so united in intimacy with Him that they form an unbreakable bond of love, which is purchased and covered by the perfect Blood of His Son, Jesus. The sacred Blood of Jesus purchases and forever seals the life-union with Him in a bond of perfect love that cannot be broken. As we remain in life-union with Jesus, His life full of glory and truth comes alive on the inside of us and draws us into greater experiential revelation of oneness with and in Him. This life-union with Jesus brings things alive in our hearts that have either been dormant or have never experienced the love of God.

Picture the perfect love of Jesus, like living water. Water has a unique ability to find *any* crack or crevice to seep into. For example, a roof on a house. Once the builder lays all the wood in place and covers it with waterproofing material, he will then cover the roof of the house with roofing tiles designed to withstand the elements of nature, such as intense heat, rain, snow, and hail. Now if there is any compromise of the roofing in the building process, when the rain or snow comes, that water will find that breach as an *invitation* and enter inside that house and begin to *saturate* everything that it touches.

Sons and daughters, we want to posture our hearts in such a tender way to the Lord, that His perfect love which flows in life-union with Him will *saturate* every area of our hearts and in our lives as we accept His invitation for more of His living water of unending love. As we abide in that life-union with Jesus, His love will work in our lives in every area that we welcome and receive Him, leading to new life, healing, and wholeness within our hearts. Abide in Jesus just as He abides in you!

Abiding Love

It is so liberating to understand that even in our worst condition of sin, brokenness, failure, and shortcomings, God still loves us with a perfect love. So, is God's love really for *you*? YES! In every stage of life and in every season, no matter the circumstances or situations, God's love is perfect for you. In these three Scriptures below, we learn Jesus completed the work that mankind never could, that the love of the Father withheld nothing and expensed everything to save us from sin. Even in our worst state of sin and darkness, His perfect love pierced and continues to pierce through to redeem us into a new life in life-union with Him.

> "For God so loved the world, that he gave his only begotten Son, that whosoever believeth in him should not perish, but have everlasting life. For God sent not his Son into the world to condemn the world; but that the world through him might be saved" (John 3:16-17).

> "This is how God showed his love among us: He sent his one and only Son into the world that we might live through him. This is love: not that we loved God, but that he loved us and sent his Son as an atoning sacrifice for our sins" (1 John 4:9-10 NIV).

> "But God demonstrates His own love toward us, in that while we were still sinners, Christ died for us" (Rom 5:8).

We see the demonstration of this perfect and incredible love of God, to have sent His only begotten Son Jesus to be the atoning sacrifice for all sin, past, present, and future, for all mankind and has removed that sin as far as the east is from the west (Col 2:13-14 & Ps 103:12). Jesus' sacrifice at the cross paved the way for humanity to be reconciled back to God in the right relationship so that we could receive His perfect love, to truly love Him and to love others as we love ourselves. This exceedingly great news of the simple gospel should come increasingly more alive in us even after receiving Jesus into our hearts as our Lord and Savior. By increasing your hunger and desire to receive more of God's love personally for you, you are pressing closer into abiding with Him as He abides in you. As mentioned above, when you do this, you will bear fruit because you are connected as one to the True Vine, Jesus Christ, as referenced in John 15:4.

Intimacy Bound

In this life of growing in receiving God's love into our hearts, we learn that our life mission is the same: for us to grow continually in love. I remember a time when the Holy Spirit spoke so clearly to me and asked me, "Will you join my IB program?" I thought to myself, "I never did any of the IB programs in school.... what is He talking about?!" I responded to the Lord and asked Him what He was asking me, and I heard Him say, "Will you join my *Intimacy Bound* program?" I immediately laughed and thought how funny and creative our God is (after all, He invented humor)! Appreciating the Lord's humor and personal love, I said to Him, "Absolutely!" I realized that the Holy Spirit was inviting me on a journey that was bound for greater intimacy with Him, and the fruit that came (and still comes) because His invitation has been life changing.

Just as the Holy Spirit gave this personal invitation to me, He extends the same warm, loving invitation to all of us all across the world! From your very conception, God made you for LOVE, and He wants you to grow in love, abound in love, abide in love, and become fruitful with love to release His love to the world. Ephesians 3:17-19 champions all of us to grow in this revelation and experience, as it says,

> "...that Christ may dwell in your hearts through faith; that you, being rooted and grounded in love, may be able to comprehend with all the saints what *is* the width and length and depth and height— to know the love of Christ which passes knowledge; that you may be filled with all the fullness of God" (Eph 3:17-19).

God made each of us not only to receive and grow in His love but also to give His love away to others, just as we have encountered Him. Your giving should always flow out of your growing as today you receive your daily bread of Jesus. If our giving exceeds our receiving and growing, most often, if not tended to, the well of one's heart can become dry just as an under-watered garden bed. Without that life source of the living water of Jesus flowing into our hearts afresh every day, our lives will become dry, leading to unrest, striving, and eventually burnout. But there is great hope.

"Your giving should always flow out of your growing as you receive today your daily bread of Jesus." [1]

— NICHOLAS BARTA

Romans 5:5 in The Passion Translation says,

"And this hope is not a disappointing fantasy, because we can now experience the endless love of God cascading into our hearts through the Holy Spirit who lives in us!" (Rom 5:5 TPT).

Imagine that for a moment. Picture yourself standing in front of an incredible waterfall on a perfect sunny day. Your heart is in complete rest with your eyes closed and your hands held out, ready to receive. Now visualize that endless cascading waterfall of the perfect love of God falling down and flowing right into your heart, filling you afresh through the power of the Holy Spirit. Not only is your 'garden bed' watered, but the soil of your soul is *saturated* with the love of God and *immersed* in His lovingkindness towards you. In pursuit of aiming towards living intimacy bound, you must not purpose to *visit* this cascading waterfall of God's love. You must position your heart to *abide* and live in the overflow.

I remember an encounter that I had with the Lord when my wife and I were traveling to southern Colorado on a wonderful trip. On that trip, we had visited a beautiful waterfall in an amazing mountain town. The sight of this waterfall was breathtaking! I can remember the cool refreshing mist of that Rocky Mountain water on that hot July day. I remember the sensation of peace and the rest of the beauty of God that surrounded that area. Simultaneously, I wanted to sit and rest and jump in the river and play, and the best part was doing both! Although I may not have realized how special and important that moment with my sweet wife and the Lord was, shortly after, I realized more depth of the spiritual significance that the Lord was teaching us through it. When we went through our pictures from our trip, we selected an amazing shot we took of that waterfall and printed a poster size print of it. The finishing touch was what the Holy Spirit spoke to us to overlay in the text at the bottom:

"Abide in the overflow." [2]

— NICHOLAS BARTA

This poster has become a memory stone for us to remember and reflect on to encourage us in our walk with God. I've found that memory stones are very handy to have around your living space, for you never know when you might need that very memory stone of God's faithfulness to champion you in your current path toward your prophetic destiny.

I think back to that incredible day from time to time and remember that cool, refreshing breeze of the water hitting the rocks on that hot summer day. This reminds me of the incredible presence and love of Jesus and how refreshing He is, even on the hottest days in our lives. This cascading endless flow of His love is always available to everyone.... including you! Receiving God's refreshing love and growing in learning new ways of continually receiving His love will point your ship towards sailing intimacy bound.

God teaches us the depth and commitment of His love towards us in Jeremiah 31:3, "The LORD appeared to us in the past, saying: "I have loved you with an everlasting love; I have drawn you with unfailing kindness" (Jer 31:3 NIV). No matter how dry you have felt or may currently feel, God will draw you towards Himself with an unfailing kindness that flows from His everlasting love personally for you. The key to accessing this love will never rest on your performance or abilities. It will always and only rest on your willingness to receive and your heart's position to abide.

Jesus teaches us about abiding love in John 15:9, where He says, "As the Father loved Me, I also have loved you; abide in My love." Abiding in the love of God can only be in learning to continually receive His love for us, being confident that the very same love that the Father has towards His beloved Son Jesus, He also has towards us because we are in Christ, and Christ is in us! We must continually draw upon and intimately receive this abiding love, allowing it to grow in and through our life's union with Jesus. The Lord Jesus commands us to "abide in My love."

This involves not a temporary, one-time receiving from the Lord at salvation or simply a here-and-there type of receiving love through periodic visitation when we feel spiritually 'deserving' or spiritually 'dry.' No, this love is constant, ever-flowing, never-changing, and always growing! Abiding in God's love will satisfy you completely, yet leave you hungry for more.... for a greater capacity to receive even more of God's perfect love intimately for you. We must choose to answer His invitation to upgrade our lives to a greater revelation of abiding in and with Him. In doing so, we're continually learning to grow in receiving God's love, which settles in our hearts where our true home really is.

Our Home is His Heart

Once again, Jesus said, "Abide in Me, and I in you. As the branch cannot bear fruit of itself, unless it abides in the vine, neither can you, unless you abide in Me" (John 15:4). The Lord unveils to all of us that our true home in this life is abiding in Him. Jesus is the very life source of life itself, and finding our home in the center of His heart brings about that revelation of what abiding truly is. In this abiding love, we not only find our true home, but we also find our central purpose in life, which is to bear fruit from living abiding in God's love.

Living in that life union with Jesus draws His fullness of life into our lives to come alive and bring life to everything we put our heads, hands, and hearts to. However, if abiding in life-union with Jesus is cut off, we strive forward in our own strength and ability that is rooted in the flesh. God's Word gives us the wisdom to know that every effort we put into something, disconnected from the True Vine, will produce nothing...nothing that will bear any fruit for the Kingdom.

Think of this like a garden hose that is watering a healthy green lawn. Now, picture that the garden hose got kinked, and there was no water flowing to nourish the lawn. As the heat of summer comes, with no water or sustenance, that green grass quickly turns brown and withers within a few short days under the intense heat of the sun. Our lives are just like that lawn, and if we abide in Jesus, His life flows like living water into every crevice of our lives, bringing life and nourishment to our souls. The result is that the 'grass' in our life will remain green and flourishing because we're intimately connected to our life source of Jesus. Yet, if we are severed from continually abiding in life-union with Jesus, not only will our lives not produce any fruit, but we will also attempt to weather the intense heat of life on our own, with no *living water* flowing into us. That leads to burnt grass and no fruit. However, Jesus promises us that if we abide in Him, we will receive His *fullness*!

God teaches us repeatedly in His Word that the key to accessing His Kingdom and tapping into that fullness is faith. As referenced earlier, Ephesians 3:17 is a key to understanding the great benefit of receiving God's love. Now, let's read it in the Passion translation.

> "Then, by constantly using your faith, the life of Christ will be released deep inside you, and the resting place of his love will become the very source and root of your life" (Eph 3:17 TPT)

This is such a powerful revelation because the Lord shows us that when we attach our faith to Him and His Word, we release the very life of Jesus deep inside us. This brings dead things to life and makes things alive and flourishing! We learn that the resting place of God's love becomes THE source and THE root of our lives. God's perfect love is the nourishment of our spirits, souls, and bodies. As we live in the resting place of His love, we live at home in His heart. Then, what we do from that place carries the life and power of Jesus into everything we put our efforts towards. The water is flowing, and the life of Jesus is alive inside of us and flowing from us to touch the lives around us, bringing about a harvest of fruit for the glory of God.

Into the Arms of Love

One of my favorite stories in the Bible regarding finding the resting place of God's love is in the parable of the prodigal sons. In Luke 15:11-32,

Jesus tells a story about two lost sons. One of which was lost and returned to the loving arms of his father. This is such a profound story and vivid imagery of the perfect heart of Father God for His sons and daughters. Although I will not be going in depth here on the parable, I highly recommend you stop and read this in the Bible for reference.

After the prodigal son, who left to spend everything, became in great need, and came to his senses, he returned to his father to become one of his hired servants. However, his plan and speech, proclaiming his unworthiness to be called his son, were pleasantly interrupted when his father sprinted toward him, pouring out compassion and wrapping him intimately in his warm, loving arms. Caught completely off guard, this prodigal son attempted his speech of declaring his unworthiness to his father to be called a son, only to be met with the father's instructions to his servants to bring the best robe to be placed on his son, sandals on his feet, a ring on his finger and a great celebration to be prepared! In a moment of time, all of this son's shame, guilt, condemnation, and unworthiness were completely wiped away by the passionate, pure love of his father.

In this very moment, this son discovered a love that saw past all of his mistakes, failures, and shortcomings. He encountered a love that was stronger than the shame and unworthiness that he felt deep in his heart. In his father's arms, all of that melted away, and this son, who was lost and locked up with guilt, then discovered his true home in the *Father's* arms. Held in those arms of love, this son experienced no shame, no insecurity, no condemnation, and no distance or separation. This lost son became fully awakened to a fullness of love greater than anything in his whole life, a love that restored, reignited, and kindled a fire of love alive in his heart that brought restoration and newfound hope.

This same love is made available to each one of us as God's children through the price Jesus paid for us on the cross. We must not only receive this love but also continually cultivate it each day in our lives, with the Lover of our souls. We can only cultivate that kind of intimacy by infinitely growing in receiving love, abiding in the true vine, and living in continual life union with Him. What we will continually discover is that God is a tender, loving Father who carefully and expertly tends to the garden of our hearts with His unfailing love that brings about greater freedom, healing, and restoration in and through our lives. We must choose to always abide and let Him tend to every intimate part of our hearts and intricate detail of our lives. It's time to let Him do some gardening in our hearts.

Worship Music to Encounter Him [3]

2

THE GENTLE HEART GARDENER
THE VOICE OF THE GOOD SHEPHERD

One of the greatest keys to living a life of abiding is prayer. Prayer has such an impact on our lives that it touches the deepest parts of who we are. In everything Jesus did, he prayed unto and with His heavenly Father. Consistently, He would withdraw from the crowds and even from His disciples to be alone and pray. Jesus would do this daily as He communed with His Abba and intimately expressed His innermost heart unto Him as He sought His Father's will in all things and in all ways. Prayer paves the road of the access points to the deepest parts of us and intimately connects them to the fullness of all of Him. Jesus shows us for all eternity that prayer is an essential part of the lifestyle of abiding. It is not simply something that Jesus did, but who He is—a person of prayer.

"Prayer paves the road of the access points to the deepest parts of us and intimately connects them to the fullness of all of Him." [1]

— NICHOLAS BARTA

As followers of Christ, we are called to be people of prayer in everything we do. Philippians 4:6-7 in the New King James exhorts us to.

> "Be anxious for nothing, but in everything by prayer and supplication, with thanksgiving, let your requests be made known to God; and the peace of God, which surpasses all understanding, will guard your hearts and minds through Christ Jesus" (Phil 4:6-7).

Here, we see that prayer is a continual aspect of life, just as it was and is for Jesus. We read here in Philippians that 'in everything,' we are to pray and make our requests known to God and to do so with thanksgiving abounding in our hearts. All throughout the gospels, we see how Jesus modeled this perfectly for us through His prayer life with the Father. Yet what we see much deeper beyond His life of prayer is Jesus' intimacy and life-union with the Father. We know that through these times of prayer, Jesus would receive direction, guidance, comfort, clarity of God's will, and marching steps for His ministry.

What this shows us is that prayer is a two-way road between us and the Lord. Just as Jesus prayed and spoke His heart and requests to the Father, He also listened to His Father's voice of love. In listening, Jesus continually heard His Father speak to Him, affirm Him, lavish love upon Him, and unveil things to come, especially Christ's pathway to the cross. All along His journey here on earth, Jesus communed with His heavenly Father daily in prayer and was filled with Father God's love, wisdom, direction, and guidance in life and His ministry.

In staying so intimately close to the Lord, Jesus taught His disciples in John 10:27 that "My sheep hear My voice, and I know them, and they follow Me." I love this verse so much because God promises us in His Word that we, as His sheep, hear His voice. There was no condition placed upon this, nor were there any limitations for only specific people. God reveals clearly to us in His Word that we ALL can hear His voice and that He intimately knows every one of us.

We may hear His voice in reading the Word, in prayer, in our dreams, in soaking (posturing our heart to listen to the Lord), or through that still small voice inside us through the Holy Spirit within us. It does not depend on us or on our performance. Through Jesus Christ, every one of us can hear the voice of God inside our hearts to lead us and guide us in the way we should go and to provide the council we need to journey onwards in life and our ministry (Ps 32:8; Isa 30:21). Jesus modeled for us what the life of abiding will always involve, which is a flourishing, unending intimate conversation with the God of all creation where we continually grow from and journey onwards in oneness with as we pursue more of Him.

Jesus, The True Vine

As we deepen our revelation of abiding with and in the Lord, we must grasp a deeper understanding of Jesus as the true vine. Jesus said in John 15:1, "I am the true vine, and My Father is the vinedresser." He unveils more in verse 5 as He says, "I am the vine, you *are* the branches. He who abides in Me, and I in him, bears much fruit; for without Me you can do nothing." When we unpack what the Lord is teaching us in these verses, what's understood may seem quite simple on the surface, yet it is beautifully profound. A branch by itself can do nothing of itself, *unless* it's connected to its life source. For us, as His branches, we must live fully from this truth that Jesus Christ is our very life source and sustenance for everything. Without remaining intimately connected to Him every day, we will gradually become dry and brittle, and eventually, we'll become detached from Life Himself. Jesus says in John 15:4 that the branch cannot bear fruit of itself *unless* it abides in the vine; therefore, neither can we bear any fruit unless we abide continually in Jesus.

Perhaps you are not a professional gardener. I certainly am not. Maybe you have never even planted anything in your lifetime. Yet, from these verses, I'm sure you can see the simplicity of what Jesus is revealing to all of us. The Lord is teaching us that a branch can *only* bear fruit *if* it is continually receiving the nutrients from its life source of the vine or tree. As a branch remains connected in life-union with the vine, then and only then can the vine transfer the nourishment of all the nutrients that it receives from the soil directly to its branches. This transference of life sustenance is continual and, of course, essential for the growth of the branch and its ability to produce fruit. A branch that is not fully connected or has a crack will not receive the complete nutrients necessary for growth and fruit production.

Now, applying this to us being the branches and Jesus being the true vine, if the branch does not connect or only has a superficial connection to the vine, it will not produce any fruit, and people will eventually remove it because it dries out, becomes brittle, and cannot withstand the challenges of life. Jesus is teaching us that unless we remain intimately joined to Him in a bond of relational love and life union, we will not have a genuine connection with Him as the true vine, and therefore, we find we are lacking His nourishment in life. From here, we find that all our efforts to produce fruit become dissatisfying and unfruitful.

I don't know about you, but I have learned this lesson the hard way more than once in my lifetime. Frequently in my past and occasionally in the present, I can remember times when I veered away from abiding and steered into striving to produce results, attempted to bear fruit through my ability and fulfill my ambitions that were actually rooted in the soil of the flesh. My soul had become dry, and I became weary as I realized that what I intended to do may have been 'good,' but working towards that 'good' goal in my strength proved fruitless and wearisome. Abba Father has taught me in these times to be aware of my sonship position unto Him and of my connection to the true vine. Through spending time in prayer with Him, He revealed the area(s) where I veered off course and pressed onwards in my ability, pursuing self-ambitions with fruitless strength. When the Lord corrected me, I found new nourishment through repentance of my errors and reconnection with my heart unto Him. As it says in God's Word, "He gives more grace. Therefore, He says: "God resists the proud, But gives grace to the humble" (Jas 4:6).

"Leave the striving and return to abiding!" [2]

— NICHOLAS BARTA

When we strive forward, endeavoring to do things in our own strength and capability while relying on our intelligence, skills, and mastery of ability in any area, we are becoming just like that branch with a superficial connection to the vine. We are not walking in an intimate sonship relationship with Jesus, and therefore, we continue toward that destination of becoming like a dry and brittle branch that is starving for Jesus' sustenance. There are far too many of us who've veered off in this direction either for a season or perhaps for a very long time. Yet there is no condemnation for those who are in Christ (Rom 8:1). The greatest joy in this place is knowing that, even if that is the case, His grace is sufficient for every one of us. It is in and through God's grace that we can find ourselves intimately joined back together in abiding in Him, receiving the life-giving source of Jesus back into our hearts, and renewing our minds. As we repent and turn away from striving to figure out life and attempting to produce fruit on our own, we will always find His grace to enable us to overcome and return to Him. 2 Corinthians 12:9 in the NIV says,

> "But he said to me, "My grace is sufficient for you, for my power is made perfect in weakness." Therefore I will boast all the more gladly about my weaknesses, so that Christ's power may rest on me" (2 Cor 12:9 NIV).

When we choose to abide in sonship and turn to the Lord in our weaknesses and inabilities, God extends us His grace and fills us with His power to overcome the challenges and hardships that we may face. Perhaps one of the greatest hurdles to overcome is our propensity to doubt, second guess, or lessen our trust in God. Even if we find ourselves in this place struggling to root deeper in our sonship unto God, God's grace is more than sufficient for us to empower us to choose to trust Him and abide in a closer relational connection with Him.

To walk more anchored in sonship here looks like first admitting our inability to figure everything out on our own. God loves to father us, and when we acknowledge our deep, continual need for His presence as Father in our lives, we are then posturing our hearts deeper in humility, which becomes a magnet that attracts His grace to empower us to grow and overcome. When we come to God as Father and yield our hearts completely over in total accountability before Him, He then leads us through our doubts and inability to trust Him and brings us to the very root of the issue where we've relied on ourselves apart from Him. In these places, if you simply take these three steps: 1. Admit your inability, 2. Acknowledge your need for Abba's fathering 3. Yield your heart completely to Him, you will then deepen your roots in sonship before God while cultivating greater trust in Him as you allow Him to father you through the lessons He's teaching you. You will be blessed with increased grace from God to overcome the hurdles of your heart that once held you back and position you to encounter His presence in new, intimate, life-changing ways.

The River of Jesus

As we press toward continually abiding in Jesus, His life flows into every space, every crevice of our lives, bringing about new life and His fullness of life to us. Revelation 22:1 in the NJKV says,

> "And he showed me a pure river of water of life, clear as crystal, proceeding from the throne of God and of the Lamb" (Rev 22:1).

As we unpack the depth of meaning in this verse, we see God has created a river of life that continually flows. The incredible revelation here is that it says that this river of life flows from the throne of God and *of* the Lamb. Wow! That river of life and pure living water is a river that flows directly *of* Jesus Christ, the Lamb of God. For all those who are connected in oneness with Him, Jesus' life flows right into their lives and into their hearts, intimately joining them together in life union with Him.

"This means that the river of life flows where you *abide*." [3]

— NICHOLAS BARTA

As you abide in Jesus, the river of His life flows into you to bring wisdom, understanding, healing, blessing, direction, counsel, and anything and everything you need in life! As you abide in the true vine, Jesus flows as a river of living water into you, providing nourishment and all sustenance needed for you as the branch to grow and produce fruit that will remain. Just as any branch cannot grow unless it is connected to its life source, so can we not grow or produce fruit unless we continually receive that living river water of the Lamb of God. The true vine contains everything your heart needs in life, and you can access it simply by abiding IN HIM. Abiding in Him will bring forth new life in our lives as we choose in our own free will to intimately come to Him as we are and receive from Him all that we need.

Come As You Are

One of my favorite sayings I once heard my spiritual papa, Dr. Leif Hetland, share was this question: "Do you need to be clean to take a bath?" For many reasons, I love this question, but perhaps most of all, because it captures people's hearts and gets all of us to see what an absurd action it would be for a person to get themselves all clean before they get into a bath or shower. I cannot think of anyone who would diligently get into the shower and fully clean themselves so they would be clean enough to take a bath (or vice versa). It makes absolutely no sense whatsoever. To have the mindset that we must be clean *before* entering the place where we get clean makes no logical sense. For it is in the shower or the bath where we go to bathe and get clean, so why would one take such unnecessary effort to clean themselves before entering the place of cleaning?

Sons and daughters, it is the same application when we come to God, thinking that we need to be clean and perfect before coming to Him. Religion has painted such a horrible picture of Christianity, where one needs to be spotless and without error in order to approach God. This is simply not the portrait that the gospels reveal to us about the heart of God. Jesus came to seek and save that which is lost, and someone who was a known sinner did not put him off or anyone who had issues (Luke 19:10). He invited all to come to Him as they are: issues, blemishes, sins, and mistakes.... all of it, and yet not one of these things put Jesus off one bit. The love flowing from Jesus embraces everyone who comes to Him, and not just at salvation. His grace and mercy flow in that river of love and are available to all who come to Him.... all who come to Him as they are, not as they think they should be.

I have seen in years of ministry that, although this may seem simple, I've witnessed many people struggle with receiving and believing this truth. Even seasoned Christians can forget the endless mercy and love of God and that He is never ashamed of us, nor is He disgusted or disappointed with us. Perhaps you have faced several disappointments in life where things didn't go as you had planned. Maybe some of these resulted from your choices, and others were results of things not in your control. Whatever the case may be, it's time to come close to Jesus as you are and have a bonfire of the disappointments and hardships that you have faced. It's time to move all barriers that have caused a breach in your intimate connection to the Lord. Without question, if we have any of these breaches in our lives, guaranteed they are issues of the heart. Proverbs 4:23 in the NKJV says, "Keep your heart with all diligence, For out of it *spring* the issues of life." I want to encourage you that wherever your walk with the Lord may be right now, there is even more of Him to discover and more of the intimate closeness with God to be lived out.

When we look to the Word of God, we learn and are reminded that Jesus' sacrifice on the cross washes, cleanses, forgives, and sets us free. 1 Corinthians 6:11 sums up this atonement work of Christ nicely,

> "And such were some of you. But you were washed, but you were sanctified, but you were justified in the name of the Lord Jesus and by the Spirit of our God" (1 Cor 6:11).

The blood of our Savior Jesus Christ sanctifies us from the world and unto God, and the finished work of Jesus justifies us as if we never sinned. There was nothing left undone in Christ's finished work at the cross! Therefore, we can carry forward with this knowledge free from all shame, guilt, condemnation, and emotions of believing that we are not good enough or that we're not doing a good enough job for the Lord. All these things attempt to sever our life-source connection with abiding in the Lord Jesus and receiving His life-giving nourishment in our hearts flowing through our lives for His glory.

What I have found in life is that sometimes these lies creep up and attempt to create a breach in that connection with Jesus, creating a block from us to receive all of Him into our lives. The simple remedy, however, is reconnecting and abiding in Jesus. Tending to the cares and needs of our hearts is the first and most important part of addressing this breach. The second part deals with our minds and thinking, which we will cover in the next chapter. The aim for now is to draw you closer to Jesus, abiding in and with Him in an unbroken flow of intimacy and relational love that leaves you forever changed, no matter how close or how far you've felt with the Lord. Psalm 55:22 in the NKJV says,

> "Cast your burden on the Lord, And He shall sustain you; He shall never permit the righteous to be moved" (Ps 55:22).

The Hebrew word for sustain is *chul* (Strong's #3557), and it means to maintain, nourish, provide food, bear, hold up, protect, support, defend, and supply the means necessary for living. As we cast the heavy burdens of our hearts that have weighed us down and caused a disconnection in our relationship with Him, He is faithful to *chul* us. The currency of exchange on our end to receive all of His benefits is to trust Him. As we cast and throw off the things of our hearts that have been wearisome, what we receive in exchange is the gentle heart Gardener who can perfectly tend to the innermost depths of our souls to bring healing, restoration, and new life. All we have to do is trust in Him and entrust our hearts completely to Him, even in the greatest places of pain, hurt, or disappointment. Jesus assures us in 1 Peter 5:7 that we can cast all our cares upon Him, for He truly and deeply cares for each of us. Now, let's respond and choose to release our cares to God and receive the invitation of the Lord, allowing the Holy Spirit to tend to the garden of our hearts.

Heart Tending

As you invite the Holy Spirit to come and intimately tend to the deepest parts of your heart, it is foundational to know and believe that He is GOOD. Let's look at just a few powerful Scriptures of the goodness of the Lord as we prepare to encounter His healing work in our hearts.

> "He loves righteousness and justice; The earth is full of the goodness of the Lord" (Ps 33:5).

"The Lord *is* good to all, And His tender mercies *are* over all His works" (Ps 145:9).

"So Jesus said to him, "Why do you call Me good? No one *is* good but One, *that is*, God" (Mark 10:18).

"Every good gift and every perfect gift is from above, and comes down from the Father of lights, with whom there is no variation or shadow of turning" (Jas 1:17).

"*I would have lost heart*, unless I had believed That I would see the goodness of the Lord In the land of the living. Wait on the Lord; Be of good courage, And He shall strengthen your heart; Wait, I say, on the Lord!" (Ps 27:13-14).

In order to trust someone, you must first believe that he or she is trustworthy. In order to trust the Lord, we must draw from the truth of His nature all throughout the Scriptures and all throughout creation that God is good all the time. This is a truth that we must never allow to be shaken by the storms and trials of life. We must never elevate our experience above His truth and the truth of who He is as a good and loving Father. We must learn to embrace the mystery of God when we have experienced loss, grief, hardship, persecution, betrayal, and death. It is in these exact times that we must draw on the truth of God's Word about His nature as good and choose to give Him worship in the places of pain, uncertainty, and loss. It is in these exact places that we can give Him something that we cannot ever give Him in heaven.... sacrificial praise amid pain.

I experienced the deliverance of God in places in my life with no answers as to why or how things happened the way they did. It was in these very places that I deeply felt and experienced the abiding nearness of God and His tender heart of perfect love that tended to the deepest parts of my soul. Even though I didn't have the answers to why things happened, I had something infinitely better.... the nearness and closeness of a loving Heavenly Father who brought supernatural deliverance of deep grief and supernatural healing to my heart. He will do the same for you and tend to the deepest parts of your heart in your life. He will bring about a rushing, flowing river of His perfect love that brings life and health to all of you! To know and to believe that God is good and to confess His goodness in your life will set a firm foundation upon the Rock that will weather whatever life may bring.

In His goodness, Abba Father tends to the deepest parts of our hearts, bringing His life alive inside of each of us. John 15:2 says, "Every branch in Me that does not bear fruit He takes away; and every *branch* that bears fruit He prunes, that it may bear more fruit." We see that Father God is the vinedresser and that His intention in pruning is to take away that which is unnecessary and does not bear fruit. We see that He also prunes that which bears fruit so that we may bear more fruit and fruit that will remain (John 15:16). In trusting in Abba Father as the vinedresser of our hearts, we can rest in trusting in Him and knowing with no doubt that He knows what He is doing, and that He is perfect at His job. As we trust Him and grant Him all access to our hearts and lives, even allowing Him to expose our greatest celebrations and our deepest fears, we know that everything He touches will flow with the river of His Son Jesus to bring healing, deliverance, and new life. Answer His invitation to take a journey with the Holy Spirit and allow Him to show you the beauty and splendor of the garden of your heart.

In The Cool of the Day

Whenever we mention a garden in the biblical sense, one can't help but picture the garden at the beginning of creation with Adam and Eve. In Genesis 3:8, we read that the Lord God walked among Adam and Eve in the garden of Eden in the cool of the day. Although the Bible doesn't explicitly state it, one can infer that it was a fairly common and regular occurrence for the LORD to walk among Adam and Eve in the garden. Can you imagine walking with God, seeing Him face to face, and talking with Him in His glory in the cool of the day?! Although we may not physically walk with God daily, we certainly can spiritually walk with Him daily in the garden of our hearts.

We strongly see the intention of the Lord in Scripture to be a guide to us and to satisfy our souls with Himself. Isaiah 58:11 says,

> "The Lord will guide you continually, And satisfy your soul in drought, And strengthen your bones; You shall be like a watered garden, And like a spring of water, whose waters do not fail" (Isa 58:11).

Here, the Lord will always guide us in the ebbs and flows of life, that He will satisfy our souls in the driest of times, and that He will provide strength to us, making us like a healthy watered garden whose waters do not cease. Thinking back to Revelation 22:1 and seeing Jesus as the river of living water for our souls, this verse in Isaiah makes much more sense for the spiritual well-being of our souls. Even though we do not physically walk with God in a literal garden on earth in the cool of the day, God's intention is that we learn to walk daily with Him in the spirit, granting Him access to all our hearts so that His nourishment can satisfy our souls.

The invitation of the Holy Spirit is for each of us to walk with Him again, as Adam and Eve did in the garden, in the cool of the day. Abba Father's heart is to be ever so intimately close to us and to be involved in every minute detail of our lives since that is what He sent His only begotten Son to redeem.... a life of unity and oneness with Himself for all eternity. As we venture deeper into His invitation to commune with Him and discover new things about God and about ourselves, we can practice cultivating this intimacy and grow in love with God as we experience Him tending to the most intimate, central parts of our hearts. It's time to walk with Him in the spirit in the garden of our hearts in the cool of the day.

Your Heart Garden

Take a moment to posture yourself in a quiet atmosphere without distractions. Set yourself in a space where you are comfortable and able to rest and relax. During this time, you can simply just be with Jesus with no concerns about tasks or thoughts of what should have been done. This is a time for you to encounter the Lord and for Him to unveil to you the beauty of your heart garden. This space allows you to explore your heart garden in the 'cool of the day' with Jesus and allows Him to show you things that you may have never known before. Before you begin, take a couple of deep breaths, breathing in Abba's perfect love for you and breathing out all stress, unrest, and anxiety. Breathe in the presence of

Jesus and breathe out all the cares of your heart to Him. Invite the Holy Spirit to come as you posture your heart unto the Lord and center your affections on Jesus.

Now, put on some soaking worship music and ask Jesus to show you what the garden of your heart is like. Welcome His presence with the affections of your heart. Ask Him to reveal to you what your heart garden looks like, and invite Him to walk with you through the garden of your heart. You may see a picture, or a movie play out in your mind or perhaps an impression from the Lord of certain things in your heart garden. The important thing here is to trust the Lord and let Him lead you however He desires to lead you in this encounter. Sit and soak with the Lord with no worries about time or results. Let Him love you and lead you in this encounter. As you see images of the garden of your heart, ask the Lord what they mean and why He showed them to you. Embrace a childlike heart filled with the awe and wonder of God alive inside you as you embrace this adventure of discovery.

Take your time, and do not rush this encounter with Him. Heaven is never in a hurry, and Jesus knows exactly what makes you tick and how you think. He is perfect at speaking the language you need to hear that will intimately connect with your heart and join it to His. Remember that you are deeply loved beyond words, and God wants to show you more of His beauty and splendor that He's placed deep inside you so that it may come to light and shine more brilliantly through you for His glory! Embrace His goodness, enjoy this journey, and journal all the Holy Spirit reveals. The river of Jesus is about to flow to the deepest parts of you as you allow His liquid love to penetrate and saturate your entire heart. Deep calls out unto deep (Ps 42:7).

Worship Music to Encounter Him [4]

3

A RENEWED MIND

THINKING THROUGH YOUR HEART

It is so powerful when we come to uncover and realize the correlation between our hearts and our minds in the way God designed us. It is truly amazing when we fathom how Father God created each of us —uniquely, intricately, and one-of-a-kind. That means that how each one of us thinks, processes, determines, and believes is perfectly unique. Now, there are endless possibilities for how we think and respond differently to situations and circumstances! What's truly astonishing is that our heavenly Father is not only able to keep track of every single one of His children's lives but also every one of our thoughts (Ps 139:2). God does this with such perfect love and tender affection, knowing the deepest parts of each one of us. It still blows my mind when I ponder how intentional and personal the God of all creation is and that He takes great delight in knowing everything about me, including precisely how I think and process life.

God teaches us something powerful about this in His Word. Proverbs 23:7 in the NKJV says, "For as he thinks in his heart, so *is* he." We learn from this Scripture that what a person thinks in his or her heart, he or she will then become. What people see within themselves and continue to think about in their hearts, they then will walk in the reality of that very thing pondered on and mulled over in their hearts. Both internal and external factors can influence a person's ability to see themselves. Often, we look at what's on the outside, which then influences what we believe and think on the inside. In order for us to align the thinking in our hearts with the truth of how God sees us, we must address how we honestly see ourselves and how well we are or are not loving ourselves. One of the most significant negative contributors toward influencing a person's thoughts within their hearts is shame.... and shame was never a part of God's intention when He gave us the ability to see and think about ourselves.

Shattering Shame to See the True You

Throughout all of creation, mankind has had the capability of seeing oneself through reflection, whether it is in a body of still water, a piece of polished bronze, or through modern-day mirrors, to name a few. God has given mankind the ability to see His most prized creation, and shame was never a part of His original design. Perhaps the Father has always desired that mankind can see His fearfully and wonderfully made creation so that we can marvel at the brilliance and inexplicable creation of the Maker and be drawn deeper into the intimate connection of abiding with Him.

Along with this freedom, God has granted mankind the ability to think independently, perceive, and formulate complex thoughts, ideas, and opinions. With this incredible freedom must also come a dependence upon His Holy Spirit to lead and guide us in our thoughts. If we do not have the leadership and guidance of the Holy Spirit in our lives, we have to rely on our own ability to see ourselves through the faulty lenses of the flesh. Through these lenses, we will certainly find distortions and disunity with the truth about who Father God says we are and how He sees and perceives us through His lenses of perfect love.

> "And *the* second *is* like it: 'You shall love your neighbor as **yourself'**"(*bold added for emphasis* Matt 22:39).

I remember a time I had learning about some of the significant implications of Proverbs 23:7 in my life when the Holy Spirit took me through a season of looking into the mirror and reflecting on what I was 'seeing' and believing in my heart about myself in the reflection. Father God had pressed into a place in my heart where I didn't realize that I had erected some beliefs about myself that didn't line up with how He saw me. To put it simply, God was taking me through a season of learning the second part of the second commandment. In Mark 12:30-31, Jesus sums up the law in two commandments, responding to the scribe's ploys when they were trying to trap Him in their law. Jesus said to them,

> "And you shall love the Lord your God with all your heart, with all your soul, with all your mind, and with all your strength.' This *is* the first commandment. And the second, like *it, is* this: 'You shall love your neighbor as yourself.' There is no other commandment greater than these" (Mark 12:30-31).

As I spent that season of looking into the mirror daily, God took me past the shame that I felt deep within my heart. The first breakthrough He brought was through shattering that shame by encouraging me to look directly into my eyes in the mirror and see the wonderful creation that I am through His perspective. As I looked into my eyes in the mirror, I began to *see* myself through my loving Father's eyes. The declaration that followed spilled out of my mouth as I muttered the words, "I love that man." Although I certainly did not like the exercise, nor did I feel anything significant about doing it initially, I reluctantly continued on. At first, I didn't really believe what I was saying, but I felt compelled by the Holy Spirit to continue to press on. The more that I practiced this exercise, the more His truth tore down strongholds of beliefs I had believed about myself and my worth.

Imagine for a moment that you can tangibly see the lies you believe in your heart. Perhaps some of these lies might be 'I'm not good enough,' 'I never measure up,' 'I never fit in,' 'I never get it right,' 'I'm not enough,' etc. Now, picture God's truth ringing loudly in your heart as you believe it in your mind. Envision these lies breaking off and being shattered at the utterance of God's truth spoken forth. Just as in this envisioning, it became true in my heart as I practiced loving myself and seeing myself the way Abba Father does. What I had not felt initially now came easily as I looked into the mirror and proclaimed the truth that I love myself and that I love the fearful and wonderful creation that I am. I believed in God's love for me and that I am loved perfectly, uniquely, perfectly, completely, and perfectly unconditionally for who I am, as God created me to be. As I believed the truth, I was speaking in alignment with God's Word. The lies and shame that once had held me back from God's truth lost their hold and were broken off. The manifestation of Proverbs 23:7 came alive and drew more fruit in my heart and through my life because of my abiding in Him.

Looking Deeper

When we look into the mirror in the modern day, we can form independent thoughts, opinions, and beliefs about what we see in the reflection. As I mentioned, the Bible teaches us in Proverbs 23:7 that "As a man thinks in his heart, so *is* he." In the Passion Translation, it says, "For as he thinks within himself so is he." Within this verse, there are two words worth looking deeper into the Hebrew language to unpack their significance further. The first is the Hebrew word for 'thinks,' which is Strong's H8175 *sha`ar* and means to split open, reason out, calculate, reckon, and estimate. The second relevant word for the study is the heart and is Strong's H5315 *nephesh* and relates to a man's soul (mind, will, and emotions), self, life, person, appetite, mind, living being, desire, emotion, and passion. When we place the significance of *sha`ar* and *nephesh* together and understand the deeper meaning in this verse, we learn that as a man or woman calculates, estimates and reasons out in their innermost being through their mind, desires, emotions, and passion, so he or she will be. Put another way, as a man reasons out and calculates in his innermost being through the activity of his mind, will, and character, so will he be.

Drawing back to the example of the mirror, we understand deeper what God is teaching us in His Word in Proverbs 23:7. What a son or daughter of God thinks and determines in his or her heart when seeing their reflection or self-perception, so shall they be. When I looked into that mirror and confronted the false calculations and reasoning that I believed within my innermost being that were not from God, I experienced the light of God's truth penetrating me at a deep level where transformation needed to take place. Here, the seed of His truth could anchor in the seedbed of my soul and bear good fruit in my life through abiding. This verse in Proverbs teaches us that the innermost thoughts of a son or daughter's life can develop into deep-seated beliefs that can dramatically direct a son or daughter's life and bear fruit thereof, be it good fruit or rotten fruit.

What a person reasons out and calculates in his or her heart can create a stronghold that reinforces and reflects either God's Kingdom or the enemy's poison in their lives in terms of what they believe about themselves. This is the place where a person creates belief systems in their mind and develops strongholds to reinforce what they deeply believe in their heart. Let's unpack on a deeper level what a stronghold in the mind is and how it's developed.

Strongholds in the Mind

I can remember when the LORD was walking my wife and me through a challenging season of relational conflict with some people in our lives. It was a difficult season of learning how to walk in unconditional love, humility, and honor while finding the balance of addressing some strongholds that were operating through this person's life and affecting our family. I can recall crying out to God in this season for reconciliation and how He had taught us many things about addressing such strongholds. One of the memorable parts of what He had revealed to me was how a stronghold tower was developed and established in the mind.

God first revealed that the initial process begins with the power of ***considering***. Let's think about the word consider for a moment. Merriam-Webster's Dictionary defines consider as 1) to think about carefully, such as 1a) to think of, especially regarding taking some action, 1b) to take into account, 2) to regard or treat in an attentive or kindly way, 3) to gaze on steadily or reflectively 4) to come to judge or classify, 5) regard, 6) suppose. For the context of this example, the definition of consider most fitting is to think carefully and to think of, especially regarding taking some action.

Take, for instance, a piece of information coming forth as a thought. Let's say, from the focus of this chapter on identity mindsets, that a person had the thought, "I failed again." This piece of information interacts with the brain, where the brain receives the signal of this information and begins the progression of considering the idea or thought. In the considering process, a person decides if the information is worth their 'appetite' and, if so, moves into the next phase.

The next step in the progression is the ***processing*** of the information. Let's say that the person decided that the thought that they failed again is worth further processing. In this process, the person thinks on the matter and develops the idea further. Perhaps some of this process is recalling the moment of failure, how it felt, what others thought of their failure, or what the implications might be. We lay the foundation of the stronghold, which becomes the ground upon which we will build the stronghold tower with further progression and agreement with the thought.

Following closely after this phase is the formulating of ***assumptions*** surrounding the processing of the thought. This could look like the person thinking thoughts like, 'I seem to fail often' or 'I just can't seem to get it right.' A person here could think over multiple other moments of failure or where they may have felt like a failure and recall the emotions that they experienced as a result thereof. Often, individuals can have memories in this place, either recent or past, that they have not resolved or where they still experience emotions of fear, insecurity, inadequacy, etc., which are brought up during this assumption-forming process. This is the place where the person independently forms these assumptions and isolates themselves from discussing it with others, especially those whom they may have a conflict with. Worth noting here is that one of the enemy's top strategies is to isolate believers away from their community and get them to process on their own, distant from God and the community. This is the phase of the thought process that is the erecting of the stones, one by one, thought by thought, that develops the building stones of the infrastructure of the stronghold tower.

Closely involved with the assumption-developing phase is the pursuit of ***searching for evidence***. The human mind is actually designed to search for evidence to support what we regularly think about and develop our belief systems around it. At this phase, there is already much infrastructure in place and a considerable amount of belief invested in the stronghold. Picture this phase as the cement that solidifies the stones permanently in place.

At this phase, the person would think further and recall other times that they failed or perceived that they had failed. A person here would think to themselves, 'I remember when I failed here' and recall how they felt. As with the assumption phase, much of the same thought process continues, but now with an added projected, devoted focus on finding evidence on how they are currently failing in their lives through their perspective. Here, this projected focus becomes toxic because the person is actively searching for evidence of how they perceive they are currently failing and building upon that negative formation of belief. Think of this as a perspective that is stained with failure so that as the person looks through those lenses, all they will see, more often than not, is evidence of failure, even if that evidence is inaccurate. If they identify enough situations and experiences as failures, they will transition into the second to last phase.

In this phase, a person is now ***establishing conclusions*** surrounding the assumptions that have developed and cemented with evidence. A person at this phase of the developing stronghold tower now establishes life conclusions on the matter at hand. Here, a person would now believe that because of the initial incident or situation of failure, supported with enough thought on the matter, reinforced with emotion, and backed by a large amount of evidence, they would conclude with the newly developed belief system that they *are* a failure, or they will *always* fail and will never truly succeed. These fortified stronghold towers can hide deep below the surface of our subconscious. This phase of the stronghold tower model is the top of the tower, firmly built upon the solid infrastructure of cemented stones on a firm foundation of evidenced thought. This is the highest vantage point and the strongest point of defense that is not easily taken over.

From here, a person only needs to transition to a further fortified position, which involves ***defending and reinforcing*** the conclusions that have erected this stronghold tower. Situations that trigger strong emotions can further reinforce the stronghold, loudly proclaiming to anyone who approaches that the person is alert and will defend their position and the conclusions they have formed. It is here that you can see a person who becomes triggered and immediately responds brashly or hyper-defensively, which, most times, isn't fully accurate or appropriate for the situation.

This is the most difficult place to break through to someone who has erected such a reinforced stronghold, yet it is the place that is most critical to have the walls penetrated with the truth of God's Word. Only then, when a person considers a truth spoken, such as in Christ, you are a success. Repenting and changing the way one thinks can take place. When this is done, we can now see that the attack of the enemy through our thoughts can be redeemed by God and repurposed with His truth for His Kingdom initiatives to be advanced in our lives.

It is here that the healing process begins! The Holy Spirit works to bring healing to areas of hurt, trauma, abuse, self-hatred, self-criticism, lack of self-love, etc. Here, through abiding, the Lover of our souls brings the nutrients of His unfailing love to those areas of our thinking and painful emotions and renews us with new perspective, insight, and Kingdom beliefs to build a new stronghold—a stronghold of Kingdom truth that is rooted in sonship!

STRONGHOLD CHART

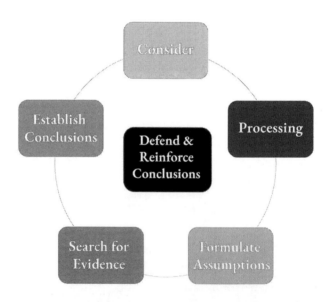

Information Consider>Process>Formulate Assumptions> Search for Evidence>Establish Conclusions> Defend & Reinforce Conclusions [1]

The Mindset of Sonship

As we deepen our understanding and pursuit to learn to live continually abiding in the Lord, one transformation that takes place is in our thinking and in the way we perceive situations in life. We are all in need of a shift in our perspective and an adjustment in our thinking—I know I sure do! Often, we believe things contrary to God and the truth of His Word. Why is that? I believe it's because of the difficult things we endure in this life, such as the losses, hurts, disappointments, pains, uncertainties, and the mystery of suffering. At these times, the human mind can sometimes try to form conclusions and give reasons and even answers to why things happened and how they did. The great danger in this is that those conclusions are based on our experiences and not on the truth of who God is and what He has said in His Word. The tension caught in between is that when we don't understand and when we do not have the answers, what will we choose to believe? These are defining moments in our lives where we can either form a stronghold of belief in our experiences or form a stronghold based on the Lord and His Word, embracing the mystery of God, and accepting that we will not know and understand everything in this life. Here is where the mindset of sonship takes root to form new thoughts and beliefs.

One of the strongest Scriptures I have found that has helped me immensely in times of tension, uncertainty, and confusion is 2 Corinthians 10:3-6.

> "For though we walk in the flesh, we do not war according to the flesh. For the weapons of our warfare *are* not carnal but mighty in God for pulling down strongholds, casting down arguments and every high thing that exalts itself against the knowledge of God, bringing every thought into captivity to the obedience of Christ, and being ready to punish all disobedience when your obedience is fulfilled" (2 Cor 10:3-6).

From this incredible verse, we learn that the major battlefield of the enemy is against our minds, attempting to infiltrate our thinking. What you believe about God is the most important thing about you. If trials and storms shake the foundation of belief in God inside of you, then the enemy can run in and sow tares of doubt, lies, and unbelief aimed to steer you away from the truth of God's nature and His Word. This is where we act on 2 Corinthians 10:5 and bring every thought captive before Jesus, trusting in Him through abiding, allowing Him to filter through the thoughts whether they are born of God, of the enemy, or the flesh.

No matter which avenue the thought comes from, you can be assured of victory with God! If it was His thought, He will bless and nurture it until it fully blossoms and bears fruit. If it was from the enemy, He'll expose it and crush the disobedience of the enemy and work with you to close the open doors from where it came from. If the thought were from your flesh, Father God would lovingly work with you and grow you to become stronger and more equipped. No matter which way it goes, the Lord has the victory for you and will bring you into a higher position of victory because of turning to Him and standing on His Word. This is the place where you can tear down strongholds of the mind that you have formed apart from God and that the enemy has generated, and you can form new Kingdom strongholds in their place.

These strongholds of Kingdom belief can be formed in our minds that become very fruitful. In order to be transformed and have a renewed mind with a new perspective, we must have a change of mind through repentance so that new strongholds of God's truth can be formed in us. God instructs us in Romans 12:2, "Do not be conformed to this world, but be transformed by the renewing of your mind, that you may prove what *is* that good and acceptable and perfect will of God." Think of this transformation and renewal of the mind like the pruning in John 15:2.

Imagine that when Jesus is referring to Abba Father, who prunes us His branches, the pruning also takes place in our minds and in our thinking. Perhaps there are 'branches' of thought in our lives that need to be taken away. Or maybe in our thinking, there has been some good fruit, but it is now in need of pruning so that we may bear more fruit in a new season with new responsibilities and new open doors of opportunity. This pruning in our minds yields better processing that grows into the maturity of thinking, like a son or daughter who remains rooted in sonship.

> "Pruning yields better mental processing." [2]
>
> — NICHOLAS BARTA

Take, for instance, our core beliefs in Christianity that originated from the truth of God's holy Word. When we posture our hearts to receive God's Word into our hearts, we then receive that seed of truth with gladness, and His Word sprouts and comes alive inside us. We add our faith in Him and in what He has spoken, knowing in the deepest parts of our beliefs that God is always good and that He is always for us. The Holy Spirit renews our mind with that which we are focusing on and believing in alignment with His Word, and the beginning of a Kingdom stronghold mindset based on truth takes hold. We then will see evidence, or fruit, of His goodness and love within and around us, and thankfulness will abound in our lives. We manifest the truth of God's goodness and love in and through our lives as a living testimony of His glory. Others get to taste and see the goodness of the Lord as we continue abiding in Jesus as our main source of life.

What it ultimately boils down to is this: you will empower in your life what you focus on most. The greatest news is that we do not need to strive on our own, trying to figure everything out and get things just right in our own ability. We have a loving Heavenly Father who fathers us through all the ebbs and flows of this life.

Living Fathered

Many years ago, I heard the Lord say to me, *"Son, if you do things using your strength, you will get your results. If you do things in My strength, you will get My perfect results."* Wow! I was in awe of what the Lord revealed to me in that season of life. I remember pondering the depths of what God was telling me as I thought about the drastic difference between those two things. What I didn't have language for then, I can now see that the Lord was highlighting the contrast between living as an orphan striving on my own versus living fully dependent as a son anchored in sonship unto Him as He fathers me through everything in life.

Even when it comes to our minds in how we're thinking and what we believe in our hearts, when we're living the lifestyle of abiding in the Lord in oneness with Him, we willfully yield to God complete access to all we are. Our minds are no longer our own. Our hearts and life ambitions are no longer our own, for we have been fused together with Christ. As we learn how to live and abide in oneness with Jesus, we then open ourselves up to become fathered by Father God in every area and aspect of our lives. We no longer are striving to figure out how and what to do in life. No longer are we battling on our own against the spiritual attacks of the enemy on our thinking or against our lives. We lean into Father God in abiding in oneness to be fathered by Him in and through everything.

For it is the Lord who brings about any transformation in our lives. We simply cannot repent and expect change and transformation apart from His hand in our lives. It is the Holy Spirit who does the incredible work in our hearts and minds that shapes us more into the image and likeness of Christ. 2 Corinthians 3:18 says,

> "But we all with unveiled face, beholding as in a mirror the glory of the Lord, are being transformed into the same image from glory to glory, just as by the Spirit of the Lord" (2 Cor 3:18).

Our portion in this transformational process in life is to anchor ever-increasingly deeper into sonship unto God and live abiding in Him as He continues to form and fashion us more into the image of His Son, Jesus. Living fathered by Abba Father is crucial in our development and fruitfulness in this life for His glory. Choosing to live in a way to be fathered by God is a choice that is rooted in a Kingdom sonship mindset. Either we have a stronghold of belief that we need to figure things out on our own, or at least some things, or we have a stronghold of belief in alignment with John 15:5 that without Him, we can do nothing. Choosing to root this core belief deep in your heart will bring forth not only fruit but also a deep hunger to live fathered by God in every area of your life. The greater depth that you believe this truth, that apart from Jesus, you can do nothing, the greater the fruitfulness and fulfillment in your life for His glory will be. Truly knowing deep in your heart that you do not need to press on in your own strength and ability should bring great freedom and joy to you.

In my experience in ministry, I have found that many adults, including fathers and mothers, have, at large, forgotten how to live fathered by Father God. Many have forgotten what it feels like to intentionally posture their hearts and lives as little children to the Father, seeking His fathering in their lives for wisdom, council, comfort, and encouragement, because of the increase in the needs of children and the responsibilities of raising them. Without question, despite your age or upbringing in life, every one of us desperately needs to be fathered by God every day and in every season of life. This is what it means to abide in and with Him in all things, and fruitfulness will abound in our lives for God's glory!

Perhaps you know this and have even lived fathered by God for a while. Maybe this is a reminder and perhaps just an invitation to welcome the Holy Spirit to search your heart and life and highlight if there are any areas where you've still strived and labored to do things on your own. I've found that these areas can remain quite hidden until Christ shines His glory light of revelation upon our hearts and reveals to us these things when we turn to Him with all our hearts. The beauty here is that if He highlights something to you, He brings the transformation and breakthrough. All He needs is our invitation to be fathered by Him, and He will do the heavy lifting with our cooperation of repentance and turning towards Him in fullness of trust in Him. By abiding closely with the Lord, we can form new mindsets, thought patterns, and lifestyles at a deeper level.

Thinking Like Jesus

As we continue to abide with Jesus in sonship, we have renewed thinking that is formed to think in the same way He thinks. 1 Corinthians 2:16 says that we have the mind of Christ, and as we abide in Him, we can think like Him. This powerful truth becomes evident when we realize that, regardless of the situation or circumstance in life, being rooted in sonship and abiding in the true vine grants us the grace and ability to think and process just like Jesus would.

I remember a time when I experienced this grace of God through my thinking when my sweet wife and I were on our incredible honeymoon. We were trying to get to Los Angeles in order to catch our international flight in time, yet inclement weather elsewhere in the United States caused the cancellation of our original flight. The service man at the counter told us we had a very small chance of catching our international flight in time because of the new flight schedule and that, most likely, we would miss our connecting flight. I decided we should go for it, and as we landed, we ran across the terminal with our luggage to get to our gate, only to find that we had missed our flight by twenty minutes. Initially, I felt so frustrated and upset this happened, but my wife encouraged me to trust the Lord. I chose to embrace that mindset of trust and declared, "I cannot wait to see how God will work this for our good!"

After we had talked to the service woman at the airline support desk, she placed us on the next flight, which didn't leave until twenty-four hours later. Being stranded in LAX at eleven at night, we continued to declare Romans 8:28, that God works all things together for our good as we trust in Him. The Lord not only provided a miracle in getting us the very last room at a nearby hotel on a Saturday night in LA, but in His grace, He provided the 'King's suite' for our honeymoon! Once we settled into our room, we messaged the hotel in Fiji about what had happened and that we would show up a day later than scheduled. We embraced everything with thankfulness as we said, "We lost a day in Fiji, but we gained a day in LA!"

We enjoyed a most wonderful day at the beaches in LA that next day, then caught our flight to Fiji that night. Once we arrived, the incredible staff greeted us with such love and apologized for our canceled flights and the lost day. The lead staff member told us they felt so bad this happened, that they upgraded us to their waterfall villa at no additional cost. We were astonished and blown away by what the Lord had done and placed on their hearts to bless us with. This villa was at least four times the amount of our budget, and in no way could we have afforded it. But God made a way, and He even fulfilled a desire of my heart as a little child to be in a house with a private pool and a moat that surrounded the home. Only God!! We enjoyed a most glorious honeymoon, to say the least, as tears of joy and thankfulness abounded from our hearts unto the Father. The

Lord upgraded our trip and supernaturally elongated our time so much that all we felt was that He had upgraded us in every way! Thank You, Abba Father!!

What I learned through this experience is that God's ways are not our ways, they're higher (Isaiah 55:8-9). I also learned that no matter the situation, when we choose to turn to the Lord and place our trust in Him, He is faithful to renew our mindset and take the situation to work for our good. My portion in this story was to change the way I was thinking and to think like a son.... like THE SON. The Holy Spirit had quickened my wife to believe and trust in Jesus and, in her beautiful faith and humility, encouraged me to do the same. God granted His grace for me to choose to think a new way about the situation, and in placing my faith fully in Him, He responded and acted upon our prayers to bring about His will to bless us. Isn't God so amazing?!

I think back to this testimony and remember from time to time when I'm facing things that appear to be impossible. I've drawn on this stronghold in my mind when facing impossibilities and remember the faithfulness of the Lord and how He's brought breakthrough, provision, and healing to areas that appeared to have no positive outcome. As a son anchored in sonship, I shaped my beliefs around what I knew to be true in my heart - that God is always good and always for us. When we understand that we truly have the mind of Christ, we can abide in Him and allow God to father us. This enables us to believe what He believes, think as He thinks, and have faith that pleases Him, even amid trials and storms. When we anchor into a mindset of sonship, we think this way: How does Father God want to come through for me in this? Who is it, Lord, that You want to be for me in this that couldn't happen outside of this set of circumstances? How are You specifically fathering me and growing me through this? What facet of Your nature are You revealing to me in this that I can come to know You more intimately?

These questions, although not exhaustive, are a starting point to help point us in directing our questions for the Lord in intimacy and relationship rather than just in the practical and logistical aspects of the situation or circumstance we're facing. Father God always wants to bring us intimately closer to Himself through abiding in everything we walk through in life. Sometimes, when we only focus our questions on the what or the how instead of the who God wants to be for us, I've noticed that we miss an opportunity to grow in a depth of love that we haven't known yet.

When we posture our hearts to be fathered by God and ask Him relational questions, I believe we grow in intimacy with Him and find the needed wisdom, direction, or comfort of the prayer of petition that we're seeking Him for. Abba Father is a Father of perfect love who will always lead us and grow us in His love all throughout our lives. It is in His love that we truly grow and become more like Christ, learning to love Him, love ourselves, and love others well. In growing in our sonship, yielding our minds over to Jesus, and allowing Him to touch, heal, prune, and grow our thinking to become like His, we then will find greater fruit in our lives and closer nearness with the Lord in our souls. As we abide in Him and continue to meditate on His goodness and faithfulness in our lives through remembering all He has done, our fruit shall be plentiful, and our leaves shall remain green and full of life.

> "I will meditate on the glorious splendor of Your majesty,
> And on Your wondrous works.
> Men shall speak of the might of Your awesome acts,
> And I will declare Your greatness.
> They shall utter the memory of Your great goodness,
> And shall sing of Your righteousness."
> (Ps 145:5-7)

4

ABIDING REST

THE SWEET FRUIT OF REST

Can you recall a time when you were at complete rest? Perhaps you were sitting on a park bench by a beautiful still lake, or maybe it was on vacation lying on the beach, hearing the waves crashing in with the cool ocean breeze. Maybe it's at one of your favorite spots to have coffee at a local shop where it's just you and Jesus as you read the Word and pray. Whatever that memory is for you, take a moment to go there in your mind. Can you picture your surroundings, the sights and sounds around you, and the sensation of rest that you feel in your heart? Perhaps the feeling of that cool ocean air blowing against your skin or the smell of that rich, delicious cup of coffee is bringing back a positive memory of a time when you felt completely at rest.

When we look at the life of Jesus, we find throughout the gospels that nothing ever rattled Him. Even when the Pharisees and Sadducees tried to provoke and entrap Him, Jesus remained in a place of complete rest and shalom peace. He responded powerfully, speaking the truth in love while not forfeiting His peace and rest for it. I can think of so many situations and life events where we grow in learning from Jesus how we are to respond rather than react to the constantly changing environment of our contemporary day. Even amid great cultural tensions with Roman rulership, oppressive regulations, and extreme taxation, Jesus did not allow Himself to be moved from abiding with the Father in perfect rest.

We learn from reading John 15 that living in the abiding produces rest. Out of that rest, we can flow and move about in this life with unwavering hope and shalom peace in all situations, just as Jesus did. However, life isn't that simple, and some situations and circumstances trigger different reactions in us where we realize we are still working out our salvation in Christ (Phil 2:12-13). This is actually an encouraging realization because it portrays that we are in process and that there is more of Jesus to discover and more of His life to come alive inside us as we continue to abide in Him. This means that living and abiding in Jesus will generate rest for our souls. Jesus is true rest, and as we live in life-union with Him, we receive the nourishment of His rest afresh in our hearts and through our lives. The key of sonship is learning to come to Him as we are to receive from Him all that we need.

Jesus said in the gospel of Matthew,

> "Are you weary, carrying a heavy burden? Come to me. I will refresh your life, for I am your oasis. Simply join your life with mine. Learn my ways and you'll discover that I'm gentle, humble, easy to please. You will find refreshment and rest in me. For all that I require of you will be pleasant and easy to bear" (Matt 11:28-30 TPT)

Yielding to Jesus all that you are and coming to Him as you are, not as you think you should be, provides an invitation for His love and rest to nourish and refresh your soul. Jesus is not concerned with who you think you are or who you think you need to be. He is passionate about receiving you as you currently are, and in fact, He gives us an invitation to come to Him when we feel weary and heavily burdened.

In John 15:4, we have learned that Jesus' continual invitation to all of His children is to come to Him and to live our lives intimately joined to Him. We learned a branch severed from Him cannot bear fruit, but only the branches that abide in the true vine will produce fruit. Perhaps the most profound revelation the Lord has shown in John 15 is that the reward of abiding in Him isn't even the fruit. Yep, that's right! The fruit isn't even the greatest result and reward of abiding in Him. The great reward of abiding in Jesus is oneness! Out of living in oneness with Jesus comes the fruit, and even the possibility of fruit that will remain long after we are gone from this earth. Therefore, we must learn to come to Jesus and to receive from Him the sweet fruit of His rest alive inside our souls.

"Be *with* Him rather than trying to get *from* Him." [1]

— NICHOLAS BARTA

We access this ability to receive from Him by placing our faith in Him. Becoming rooted in sonship will burn the desire deep in your heart to pursue being *with* Him rather than trying to get *from* Him. Through abiding, all of Him is made manifest and available to all of you. God withholds nothing of Himself, but gives all of Himself to us to be joined as one in glorious oneness. Learning that all of Him is already available to you will draw you into a deeper place of trusting in God to provide for your every need, especially your deepest need for His rest alive in you.

Rest For Your Soul

Your heart is the most important part of you to be stewarded. It is the place where we can receive from and be released from, and it is, according to Scripture, the most important place to be guarded (Prov 4:23). His rest resides in our hearts and flows unrestricted from us as we continue to abide in Jesus, our true rest. God graciously teaches us that out of our hearts flow all the issues of life, so can you imagine the immeasurable significance of posturing our hearts to receive and to be at continual rest in Him?! To be *at* rest, we must live *in* rest with Him. Living in rest with Him will always involve an exchange of the busyness of our minds and hearts for the pure flowing love of Jesus alive in us.

"To be *at* rest, we must live *in* rest with Him." [2]

In Matthew 11:29, Jesus reveals He is the provider of rest for our souls. In The Passion Translation, we discover Jesus is our oasis, our place of refuge and retreat to come away and be with Him and find that rest that we so desperately need. It is in this very place of abiding in Him that His rest fills our souls and overwhelms the places in our hearts where we have been feeling weary and heavy-laden. The great news about Jesus being our place of refuge is that no matter where we are, we can access that place of oasis because He lives in us through His Holy Spirit. Therefore, we carry that refuge of rest everywhere we go because we're one with Him! There's no place of restriction for Him, yet all He needs is an open invitation from our hearts to come in. Even if we are feeling burned out, heavy, and weary in life, these are the exact places where Jesus desires to come in and commune with us in intimacy to restore us unto Himself. No matter how heavy or how weary you feel in this life, Jesus will always provide spiritual rest for your soul.

His Light Yoke Upon You

I remember a time experiencing that oasis of Jesus as I was on a mountain bike ride. It had been a challenging season, with many things going on in life. I went for a ride, consciously inviting the Lord's presence alive in my heart as I went. I enjoyed the thrills and joy of exploring the new terrain as I biked around, enjoying the beauty of God's creation.

At one point, the Holy Spirit prompted me to stop and rest in Him. I felt His presence overwhelm me as He washed His rest over me. The wind began to blow a cool autumn breeze gently against my body, and I felt the sensation of His rest filling my heart afresh as I continued to receive Him with all my heart. I closed my eyes and tilted my head back in a posture of rest to receive Him. There was nothing I did to earn this or to be particularly spiritually prepared to receive this encounter with the Lord. All I did was turn all my affections toward God and, in faith, press my heart further into Him through abiding. Before I knew it, Jesus' rest completely overwhelmed my soul. My heart was at ease, and my mind was at peace. I did not feel stressed or concerned about all the other things that were going on in life. I simply felt as if Jesus placed His yoke upon me and granted His rest for my soul. When I became more aware of what Jesus was doing in my heart, I sensed the Holy Spirit rephrase a concept from Matthew 11:28-30 as,

---

"His yoke is LOVE." [3]

— NICHOLAS BARTA

As I processed more about the encounter at a later time, God taught me more about what His yoke is. When we are abiding in Christ, He promises to give us His yoke that is easy. The wildest part about His yoke is that He lavishes it and soaks it with the oil of intimacy with Him. The funny thing about oil is that it is very slippery. When we are abiding in Jesus and coming to Him with all the affections of our heart, He places that yoke of oily, slippery intimacy upon our shoulders where the cares and weights of this life seem to just slip right off of our shoulders. Jesus' yoke is love that He places upon us to lead and guide us in this life. It is not a heavy wooden burdensome yoke to weigh us down and cause us to stumble. No, His yoke is so easy that it fills us as He fits it upon us. As we are abiding in oneness with Him, we find that His oil of intimacy is the most effective yoke against the trials, hardships, and cares of this life. Here, we find that a beautiful exchange takes place, our worries and heavy burdens for His easy yoke and burden of light.

I remember a time many years ago when the Lord was speaking to me about this verse. He asked me the question regarding 'His burden is light' and said, "Son, how heavy is light? Immediately, amazement overwhelmed me as I grasped a revelation I had never seen before in this passage. Realizing that there probably was no way to quantify the answer to if and how much light weighs, I responded, "Surely You know, Lord." Jesus' response to me was, "Exactly! "MY yoke is easy, and MY burden is *light*." I was amazed in the Lord, for I had never even thought about His burden being literal light, the glory light of Christ, that surrounds us and never weighs us down.

With your heart positioned in sonship and opened to receive from Jesus, He will then lavish you with His yoke of love that will surround you, fill you, and guide you in every step of this life with His unending love. It is from His yoke of love that we learn from Him, adopting His ways of doing things and His way of responding to things in life. We learn rest as we receive His yoke of love, and that very rest then becomes expressed in and through our lives to produce fruit. In His yoke, we learn His perspective of love, the response of love, the mindset of love, and the lifestyle of love—all found through abiding!

As our hearts and minds become transformed by His yoke of love resting alive in our hearts, the manifestation of His love increases in and through our lives, producing that fruit for His glory. Jesus' yoke of love then replaces all the heavy yokes we have experienced that have kept us from living at rest. All the stresses we felt, the frustrations we've expressed, the hardships we've endured, and the uncertainties we've faced have melted away with the authority of Christ's rest abiding in our hearts. Through this continual receiving, the Holy Spirit teaches us day by day how to manage our hearts and to live out of that spiritual rest found through abiding. Then, when unexpected things come our way, we see the fruit of responding like Jesus would in challenging situations and trying circumstances. Learning to manage our hearts and anchor deeper in rest in the Lord is an absolute necessity in these last days and an essential part of accessing His victory in our lives.

Victory From Rest

There are many depictions and stories from the Bible where God teaches us not only the importance of rest but also the victory found in abiding in His rest. The authority of God's love is most powerfully released through us when we are living in His rest. You are at your best when you're living in His rest. Psalm 110:1 says, "Sit at My right hand, Till I make Your enemies Your footstool." This Scripture's first and most notable revelation is knowing that it is in Christ Jesus, first, that all enemies have been made His footstool. Since we are in Christ and Christ is in us the hope of glory, we too will see our enemies made to be our footstools (Col 1:27). Second, we see in this verse that God is calling us to 'sit' at His table, which is a posture of rest. As we rest in Him and place our faith in God's ability and not in our own, we are exchanging striving for abiding and are living in a place of victory from worry, doubt, fear, etc.

> "You are at your best when you're living in His rest." [4]
>
> — NICHOLAS BARTA

If you find yourself in a place of worry or doubt, the number one way to pursue victory over the situation is to turn and repent. True repentance from the heart breaks the hold that fear or sin once held, and it makes the runway for freedom and victory to take off in your life. Fear, doubt, worry, anxiety, stress, unbelief, heaviness, and weariness are some of the many enemies of rest. Dealing with these through repentance and the Blood of Jesus makes the heavy work easy. What is required of us in exchange is that we place our trust, confidence, and faith in God alone in the situation, placing all the chips in His lap with no plan B held in our hearts. Here, we live surrendered, truly trusting God to come through for us. It is here also that we can experience some of the most powerful rest—a table where we sit, eat, and rest in the presence of all our enemies.

> "You prepare a table before me in the presence of my enemies; You anoint my head with oil; My cup runs over" (Ps 23:5).

The depth of trust in God, which remains unshaken by the trials of life, is where this type of victorious rest is found. It is a place of authority that trumps the impossibilities of life and brokers forth Christ's eternal victory into the situation. This is the place where Jesus desires His children to learn from Him and to take His yoke of love upon them and live at rest, no matter what life brings before them. Psalm 46:10 says, "Be still, and know that I *am* God; I will be exalted among the nations, I will be exalted in the earth!" God reveals to us that in our being still, meaning at shalom peace in Him and in trusting in Him, we are to know in all ways and in all things that HE is God. We find true strength in the stillness. In the stillness, we are at rest in the knowledge of knowing that God is the only one who rules and reigns over all creation and all the affairs of men. Here, we learn increasingly more of what it means to live at rest in the Lord and to trust in Him to bring victory to our situations in life. It is in choosing to be still and know that He is God that we confess our faith and anchor deeper into trusting Him, that He responds to our faith and gives us His rest—even rest in the battle.

"In the stillness, true strength is found." [5]

— NICHOLAS BARTA

I remember a time when I was on a virtual call with people around the world. The presence of Jesus came so powerfully after we had prayed that His glory filled the atmosphere in everyone's homes. It was the most incredible sensation in God's glorious presence as He filled each of us with His rest in His glory. We shared Psalm 46:10, and God's manifest glory increased. Everyone lingered in God's presence, receiving the nourishment of His living river of love deep inside our hearts. No one spoke for many minutes, and there was no concern for what time it was. I remember that after the call ended, I could only put on some soaking prayer music and be with Jesus.

In that encounter, He strengthened and filled my soul with His rest and victory. I felt encouraged and uplifted in the divine exchange that took place, and the encounter continued throughout that week. In His immense, infinitely expansive grace, He taught us all more of what it meant to abide and be with Him in rest. In this rest, God's victory became manifest to me and to all on that call. The beauty was that there was nothing needed to strive for to attain it; rather, it just came as fruit from abiding.

From Striving to Thriving

Of all the spiritual battles I have faced in my lifetime, I've learned that the most powerful position in warfare has been the position of rest. As I shared earlier in this chapter, when we look at the life and leadership of Jesus, we see He allowed nothing to move Him out of the place of abiding with His Father in perfect rest. He calls each of us to live in the same way and to trust in Him for everything in life. When we choose to live this way and posture our hearts to receive His yoke of love and rest, we then learn to pray with great authority from a position of His rest. Instead of striving in our human efforts to battle through spiritual difficulties and challenging circumstances in our flesh, we are turning to Father God and abiding in Jesus to produce supernatural fruit that yields supernatural results.

It is right here in sonship where we learn to live as sons and daughters with a great BIG Father who is infinitely capable of providing for our every need. This is the place where we transition away from striving and into abiding, which will eventually lead us to thriving in life! As we learn to enter the rest that Jesus won for us, in sonship, we no longer are looking to ourselves to be the providers of solutions to the problems we face and the difficulties we endure. We deepen our roots of abiding in Christ Jesus, our hope of glory, to live through us and bring His Kingdom into every situation.

It is no longer you who live, but Christ in you, and Christ through you, to bring about the victory. We no longer place confidence in the flesh but place our confidence solely in Him, which yields great reward (Heb 10:35-36). It is by living in oneness through abiding that we access the place of fullness of His victory in our lives, trusting in Him no matter the results, knowing that He is good and that He is God.

As we enter Christ's rest that He won for us, we will see greater fruit and greater victory in our lives for Jesus' glory and honor. Hebrews 4:1-10 talks about that spiritual rest that Jesus won for us, and God promises that Christ's rest is for each of us in verse nine, which says, "There remains therefore a rest for the people of God." As you deepen your roots in sonship and abide continually in Jesus as your true source for everything in life, you will yield the fruit of His perfect rest alive in your heart and manifesting in your spirit, soul, and body. The striving of the flesh is replaced with the thriving in the spirit as you walk by the spirit and not by the flesh to see Christ's victory flowing in you and through you for His glory. Learning to steward our hearts well this way becomes the pursuit as Jesus shines in you and through you for others to see His goodness. Faithful stewardship leads to fruitful increases as we cultivate His living Word that's deposited in us.

Worship Music to Encounter Him [6]

5

THE PARABLE OF PARABLES
THE PARABLE OF THE SOWER

One of my favorite things about Jesus, whenever He preached, was that He usually did thorough storytelling. Jesus shared parables that excited people and caused them to think and ponder the depth of what He was sharing to unveil the applicable meaning behind what was being shared. So often, Jesus shared parables with significant spiritual meaning and life application. In doing so, these parables would confound the wise, hoping they would turn from reliance on their own intellect and flesh-filled wisdom and turn to God, relying on Him as little children capable of learning the meaning and spiritual life application behind the stories that He would share. Jesus even stated joyfully unto His heavenly Father in Matthew 11:25-26,

"At that time Jesus answered and said, "I thank You, Father, Lord of heaven and earth, that You have hidden these things from the wise and prudent and have revealed them to babes. Even so, Father, for so it seemed good in Your sight" (Matt 11:25-26).

Through this, God intends to woo His children into a place of childlikeness and dependence rooted in sonship unto Him as we turn away from independence and self-reliance rooted in the flesh. God hid the mysteries of His Kingdom's reality and revelation from the wise and prideful. Yet,

He gave them to the spiritual babes of the faith who would humble themselves, seek God, and rely on Him as Father to reveal the beautiful mystery of His Word and His Kingdom.

Jesus rejoiced that His Father had chosen to reveal the great mysteries and revelation of Himself and His Kingdom to spiritual babes who depend fully on the Lord and put no confidence in the flesh (Phil 3:3-9). We see that this exchange requires us to fully surrender our brilliance, knowledge, wisdom, and intellect to God's supreme Lordship. It is in acknowledging our need for God and to receive the gospel that our hearts become softened, and our minds become open to the King and to the mysteries of His Kingdom (Mark 4:11). The heart of sonship acknowledges that apart from Jesus, we can do nothing and that we are as nothing without Him since He alone is our life source.

Of all the parables that Jesus shared, there was one that He stated was key to understanding all parables (Mark 4:13). As we dive into what Jesus referred to as the parable that is essential to understanding all parables, we learn a great depth about what it means to abide in close relationship and oneness with God, co-laboring with Him to steward all that He has given us. In doing so, we receive the blessing of the revelation of the mysteries of God through a clear understanding of His Word. Now, let's dive into this great parable.

> "Listen! Behold, a sower went out to sow. And it happened, as he sowed, *that* some *seed* fell by the wayside; and the birds of the air came and devoured it. Some fell on stony ground, where it did not have much earth, and immediately it sprang up because it had no depth of earth. But when the sun was up it was scorched, and because it had no root it withered away. And some *seed* fell among thorns; and the thorns grew up and choked it, and it yielded no crop. But other *seed* fell on good ground and yielded a crop that sprang up, increased, and produced: some thirtyfold, some sixty, and some a hundred." And He said to them, "He who has ears to hear, let him hear!" (Mark 4:3-9).

As Jesus shared this parable, we learn that even His disciples were confounded about the interpretation of the parable. They were clueless, yet hungry for the revelation of the meaning behind it. Yet, one very distinct thing separated them from everyone else. They had *access* to the Lord to inquire of Him to receive the revelation behind what He was speaking. As born-again believers filled with the Holy Spirit of God, we too have *access* to Him and to receiving the revelation of His Word alive in our hearts. To receive that revelation and wisdom from God, we must humble ourselves of all reliance on our own abilities and become as little children with a great big Father who knows how to come to Him and receive from Him as beloved sons and daughters. As we deepen our root system in Him through abiding in Him, we will find even greater fruit. Abiding in the Lord yields wisdom, understanding, and direction. The Lord's heart is that we seek those things out by living and abiding in the true vine.

This parable is key because it is about receiving the Word of God in our hearts. It is not only about how we receive the Word and revelation of God, but also how we *steward* it. Now, let's read what Jesus revealed to His disciples who were abiding with Him.

> "And He said to them, "Do you not understand this parable? How, then, will you understand all the parables? The sower sows the word. And these are the ones by the wayside where the word is sown. When they hear, Satan comes immediately and takes away the word that was sown in their hearts. These, likewise, are the ones sown on stony ground who, when they hear the word, immediately receive it with gladness, and they have no root in themselves and endure only for a while. Afterward, when tribulation or persecution arises for the word's sake, they immediately stumble. Now these are the ones sown among thorns; *they are* the ones who hear the word, and the cares of this world, the deceitfulness of riches, and the desires for other things entering in choke the word, and it becomes unfruitful. But these are the ones sown on good ground, those who hear the word, accept *it*, and bear fruit: some thirtyfold, some sixty, and some a hundred" (Mark 4:13-20).

As Jesus reveals the spiritual application and revelation of this parable, He highlights four main areas that depict the possible conditions of our hearts and our capability of receiving His Word. Jesus was using these four areas, the wayside, stony ground, thorns, and good soil, as metaphors for the condition of the soil of our hearts and our ability to receive the planting of His Word. God Himself is the sower and sends His anointed ones to us to sow His Word into our hearts. The question at stake for all of us is, what is the desire and appetite of our hearts in relation to *receiving* the Word of the Lord? We must continually examine that in our hearts before the Lord throughout our lives in abiding with Him. Only the Holy Spirit, the Spirit of all truth, can reveal the condition of our hearts and water the soil of our hearts to soften them to become like good ground where we joyfully hear and receive the Word of the Lord. So, what's the condition of the soil of your heart?? Jesus is showing us that this very condition of our hearts has a direct and essential correlation to our ability to receive His Word and Kingdom revelation into our hearts, thus following our ability to steward and multiply it for His glory.

As Jesus used the wayside as His first metaphor for the condition of man's hearts, we can learn a great deal about what that means for us as His disciples living in our contemporary day. By unpacking the Greek word for 'wayside' (Strong's G3598), it's unveiled that it can refer to "a course of conduct" or "a way (i.e., manner) of thinking, feeling or deciding." When I think of the word wayside, I envision something on the side of the road, which is off the desired or intended pathway. When we pull in the revelation of the Greek, we see that the appetite of our hearts to think on, have feelings towards, and desire the word can impact our ability, or inability, to receive the seed of God's Word into our hearts. Jesus shares that the ones whose hearts have fallen by the wayside hear the Word of God, and Satan immediately takes the seed away.

Our manner of thinking and the attitude of our hearts towards receiving the seed of God's Word play a direct role in its destination for it to be firmly planted or snatched away. Leaving an attitude or way of thinking that is lukewarm, careless, or inconsiderate to the Word of God will leave us vulnerable to the birds of the air to come and devour the Word before it can ever be sown and take root in our hearts. Jesus is showing us that when we are casual and do not direct our hearts to hear and hungrily receive His Word with gladness into our hearts, we too fall by the wayside, and what was sown becomes snatched away, therefore having no chance of bearing any fruit. If our heart has wandered away from abiding and is lacking in reverence and spiritual appetite to receive God's Word, then that is when we begin to fall by the wayside.

The second metaphor Jesus used is the stony places that had little earth available for ideal planting and rooting. These are the ones who hear the Word of the Lord and receive it with joy, yet because of the lack of the desperate need for deep roots, these only endure for a time. The revelation of the roots correlates with our intimacy with Jesus. If we do not have a strong, deepening relationship with the Lord being continually cultivated in our hearts, we cannot endure when the heat is turned up. In the first metaphor, we see that the soil of our hearts, in terms of our attitude and spiritual hunger to grow, is unveiled. This second metaphor brings the root system of our intimacy with the Lord to the forefront.

Without continually deepening our roots of intimate love with the Lord, we will not have the root system necessary to endure the heat that increases because of the Word being deposited. Notice how the rest of Mark 4:17 says, "Afterward, when tribulation or persecution arises for the word's sake, immediately they stumble." The key emphasis here is *"arises for the word's sake."* God teaches us here that there will be times of tribulation, hardship, tension, difficulty, and even persecution that will arise for the testing and warfare over the Word being deposited. We know that the enemy Satan, battles against the saints being raised up in the Lord and walking out our God-given destiny. However, a son or daughter of God who has pressed deep into abiding with the Lord, cultivating close intimate relationships and oneness with God, will be capable of enduring the times in life that are difficult when that word is being battled against and tested for its depth.

Has there ever been a time in your life when you have received a prophetic word from the Lord, where another believer spoke words of destiny over your life? Maybe they received something from the Holy Spirit and saw a part of who you are in God's eyes and what He's given you to deposit on this earth for His glory. Perhaps after receiving such a word, you entered a time of hardship and spiritual warfare. Or maybe there was a time sitting in church, hearing a sermon, reading the Word of God, or reading one of your favorite devotions, and the Holy Spirit unveiled a deeper revelation of His Word to your heart. Perhaps shortly after that time, there was an opportunity in disguise of testing that word through the fire of tribulation or persecution where God was taking what the enemy meant for evil and turning it for your good for the word's sake to be deepened in you and strengthened within you. These are the times in our lives when we must press deep into abiding with Jesus so that His word does not merely spring up in our hearts with joy in one moment, then in the next moment be scorched by the heat since we did not press our roots of trust, intimacy, and connection deeper into the Lord.

> "Trust in the Lord with all your heart, And lean not on your own understanding; In all your ways acknowledge Him, And He shall direct your paths" (Prov 3:5-6).

I love this verse for many reasons, but one of the most significant reasons is the revelation of sonship. We must understand throughout this life that in and of ourselves, we can do nothing without Him. As shared earlier in this chapter, we must lay down all of our intellect and our own ability to understand, comprehend, and formulate conclusions. We must choose to trust in Jesus despite all the things we do not understand and have no answers to. Just as we see in this verse in Mark 4:17, there *will be* times of battle and tribulation for the sake of that word of the Lord taking deep root within the soil of our hearts and bearing fruit in our lives. Yet it is in the very trials of life where our faith is forged in the fire. It is in the resistance that comes against the Word that our spiritual muscles are formed and strengthened. Father God, in His absolute goodness, will take that resistance, persecution, and tribulation to strengthen us and equip us to bear fruit for His glory, even in times of spiritual drought and hardship. Persecution produces faith in the saints, and a strong root system of intimacy with Jesus will produce fruit of forbearance even during the driest of times. Let our hearts not become as stony ground with no roots sustainable to retain the word of the Lord, but rather that our hearts would be a well-watered garden (Is 58:11), flourishing with roots of deep intimacy with God.

> "And not only *that*, but we also glory in tribulations, knowing that tribulation produces perseverance; and perseverance, character; and character, hope. Now hope does not disappoint, because the love of God has been poured out in our hearts by the Holy Spirit who was given to us" (Rom 5:3-5).

The final condition of the soil of our hearts is the most prevalent in our world today. We see thorns every day in our contemporary culture. In my nation, we continually see billboards and advertisements that attempt to persuade people that their lives will be better and more fun if they buy this product, drive this type of car, eat this kind of food, and drink this kind of drink. We are continuously surrounded by opposing desires and lusts of the world that directly attempt to compete with God's Kingdom, alive and thriving in us. We are as wheat sown among the tares of the world.

Jesus warns us about these thorns and the impact they can have in our lives to choke out the word of the Lord from bringing life from within us and springing forth from us. When the cares of the world take up residence within our hearts, the spiritual appetite of our hearts lessens as we choose to place the world's delicacies on our spiritual palate and find them appealing and desirable. When our pursuit of riches, wealth, the increase of possessions, and influence become more significant than our appetite for the Lord and to receive from Him continually, the potential for fruitfulness in our lives becomes choked out. These thorns become a blockade within our hearts that prevents us from hearing and receiving the truth of God's Word deep within our hearts, that would have eventually produced fruit for God's glory.

Jesus said in Matthew 6:24, "No one can serve two masters; for either he will hate the one and love the other, or else he will be loyal to the one and despise the other. You cannot serve God and mammon."

There is a cost to following Jesus and to pressing into more abiding in Him. That cost is forfeiting the delicacies of the worldly system and the intentional pursuit of riches and wealth apart from Christ being the center of our affections and devotion. For our lives to become fruitful, be it thirtyfold, sixtyfold, or a hundredfold, we must posture ourselves daily in welcoming the Holy Spirit till our hearts become like the soil of the good ground.

Jesus contrasts the fourth soil drastically with the good ground being the only one that yielded a crop and bore fruitfulness. The good ground is the only place to find real production and multiplication. While Jesus was sharing this parable, He was tilling the ground in people's hearts to receive the seed of the word He was releasing. There was awe and hunger in the hearts of His disciples, who pressed into that relationship to receive the revelation of the words of Jesus, hoping their lives might be worthy of bearing fruit for the Lord.

Jesus shares so clearly in this parable that the posture and attitude of the heart, the root system of intimacy, and the alignment of the desires of the heart are all needed for the acceptance, harboring, and growth of the Word of the Lord in and through our lives to produce fruitfulness for Him. With none of these essential spiritual truths alive in our walk with God, it is doubtful that fruitfulness can abound. In abiding in Jesus, we learn His ways of tending the soil of our hearts, weeding out any worldliness and flesh-orientated pursuits. Jesus unveils the life of sonship by showing us the impact of the soil of our hearts in relation to different life situations that can arise. Only by abiding in Him can we truly receive from Him so that the fruitfulness of oneness can abound in our lives.

In all three synoptic gospels where the parable of the sower is found, the bookends remain the same, while the center of the text differentiates slightly. This is because the Lord highlights that the heart of the matter is the key to hearing, receiving, and multiplying His Word in and through our lives. Notice the key words used in the same parable in Matthew, Mark, and Luke:

> Matthew 13: Hear, Understand, Bear Fruit
> Mark 4: Hear, Accept, Bear Fruit
> Luke 8: Hear, Keep It, Bear Fruit

All synoptic gospel accounts deal with our spiritual appetite to receive, accept, and keep, holding them close to our hearts, finding them desirable and valuable, and pursuing understanding to, therefore, bear fruit. The remedy is to have ears to hear the Word of the Lord, hearts to receive and accept it, a mind that yields to Christ and seeks Him to understand it, and a willingness through sonship to bear fruit and multiply it for God's glory!

Jesus commands and gives directives to us that we must hear and have ears to hear what the Lord is saying to His beloved people. We cannot hear with our presumptions, conclusions, or faulty flesh. We must hear with our hearts that are postured on the Lord and reliant upon Him to give our hearts and minds the understanding of what He is speaking. Then, when it deals with our hearts, we must accept the word, keep it treasured in our hearts, and lean in to understand what God is speaking to us. From there, Jesus' command is straightforward: bear fruit! Go and share the seed of the Word that has been received! Be a generous, contagious Christian who, after hearing a fresh word of the Lord or being given a revelation from God's Word, then goes out and sows it into the hearts of others who will also receive and multiply that word. This is the way of the Kingdom: "Freely you have received, freely give" (Matt 10:8). Bearing fruit for the Lord is not intended to be stored. It is poured, poured out, and multiplied in the lives of those around us. Most importantly, before multiplying the word, bearing fruit can only come from one source—abiding.

The Word Abiding In You

In John 15:7, Jesus said, "If you abide in Me and My words abide in you..." Let's think about that for a moment. It is evident that Jesus clearly highlights the importance of His words continuing within us. Not only are we to abide in Him always, but we are also called to allow His words and Word to abide within us continually. This is key to bearing fruit and also to recognizing the voice of the Lord when He speaks. Just as Jesus said in this parable, "He who has ears to hear, let him hear!" (Mark 4:9), our ability to hear Him with our whole hearts is directly tied to our ability to love Him with all our lives. When we love the Lord with all our hearts, even if He is sharing some difficult things with us, we can remain confident in our Knower, Jesus, that His intentions are always for our good.

God portrays this truth perfectly in Hebrews 3:15, "Today, if you will hear His voice, do not harden your hearts as in the rebellion."

One of the most obvious but far too neglected ways we can grow in attuning our ears to hear the Lord is reading His Word. As we read the Bible, we are attuning our hearts and spiritual ears to recognize God's voice in our lives. The more we read His Word daily with the heart of sonship, the more we become intimate with God and understand His ways. As we continue abiding in Him and allow His words to abide in us, we are continually being transformed more into His image and likeness, and our spiritual hearing becomes sharpened to hear the word of the Lord with increased hunger, clarity, understanding, and discernment. By the grace of God through the Holy Spirit inside of us, we are gifted with the ability to hear, then accept, keep, understand, and eventually bear fruit for God's Kingdom. These first flow from us abiding in the true vine of Jesus in relational intimacy, allowing His words to remain alive inside our hearts and flowing out of our mouths and through our hands for His glory. Now, that sounds like good fruit from a pure vessel that will remain!

Tilled & Prepared To Receive

The softening of the soil of our hearts can only come from remaining close to Jesus, growing in our trust in Him, and allowing His Holy Spirit to work within our hearts to weed out all that does not belong. The soil of our hearts is tilled and prepared in the abiding **to receive the word** of the Kingdom deep into our hearts so that it can be multiplied and bear much fruit: thirtyfold, sixtyfold, or a hundredfold. When we abide in a close life union with Jesus, we strengthen our trust in Him that is not conditionally based on our own understanding of the disappointments and hardships we face. When we abide, we are open, and when we are open, we can hear the word of the Lord and receive it into the good ground of our hearts.

Truth be known, our hearts are like a gate where we choose what we allow in and keep out. When there are difficulties in life that we do not understand, namely the 'heat' we face in life mentioned earlier, our ability to endure through those times of challenge will be directly correlated to our abiding in the Lord. Our abiding in the Lord will draw our hearts open to receive a fresh revelation and word of the Lord in our time of need. It is in these very times of hardship where the word of the Lord is most strengthening, and I believe perhaps the most fruitful.

Here in the United States, many species of pine trees in the mountainous areas shed pinecones throughout the year. However, one fact about a specific species of pine trees remains incredible to me. Particularly, Jack pine, Lodgepole pine, and Table Mountain pine trees have an amazing ability to produce serotinous pinecones that are unlike any other. These serotinous cones are thick and are covered with a strong resin that enables them to remain 'glued' shut and attached to the pine tree branches for years. When there are times of drought and the immense heat of forest fires spread quickly and rapidly, these cones hold their seed protected tightly and securely deep within and secured by the strong resin. Yet when a fire sweeps through a forest, the intense heat eventually melts away that resin and breaks open the *opportunity* for those seeds to be released and carried by the wind or by gravity so that they become planted and multiplied. In some ways, these pines depend upon *fire* to produce seed and multiply.

You see, the very heat intended to destroy these cones is the very thing that opens them up to be fruitful and to multiply. Just as we read in the parable of the sower, when hardship arises *for the word's sake*, we can remember this real application through God's nature, that the very heat of life will strengthen the word and be used by God to multiply it so that it may produce fruit for His glory. May our hearts be lavished with the resin of the Holy Spirit so that the seeds of the words of God are held deep and close within our hearts and shared with others to bear fruit for God. When the heat is turned up in life, may those very times be the prime opportunity for the seed of the Word of God in our hearts to be strengthened, opened, and spread rapidly to produce fruit. The Lord takes whatever the enemy meant for evil and turns it for our good (Rom 8:28).

Fruit On The Journey

The ambition and intention of the Lord for all of His children does not differ from what He spoke to Adam and Eve in the garden after He had released His blessing and commissioning upon them: "Be fruitful and multiply..." (Gen 1:28). This commissioning carries on forward to all of us today because God's Word never returns void (Isa 55:11). We are all called to be fruitful, and not merely fruitful in our end result, but fruitful along the journey. We are called to release what we carry of all that has been given. Great receivers will become great releasers. Only what we have received can we truly give. What we give freely and selflessly will always be multiplied by God when our ambition is anchored in love and intended for His glory. Remember the boy with the two fish and five loaves? This young boy's love and selflessness were used by God to feed well over five thousand people, all out of simple obedience to release what had been given to him (John 6:1-14).

"Great receivers will become great releasers." [1]

— NICHOLAS BARTA

Just like this little child, we too are called and blessed by God to be 'fruit-FULL' and multiply all that our good Father has given us to steward. Perhaps most relevant is that the mindset of 'consumer' must transition to become a mindset of 'multiplier.' Only then are we moving away from storing up treasure for ourselves and moving towards spending our oil at the holy, sacred feet of Jesus! Like an alabaster jar full of costly fragrance, may our hearts be full of intimacy with Jesus so that we can faithfully steward and multiply all God has given us and pour it out upon those all around us. We must hear, receive, steward, and multiply all He has given us to be faithful and fruitful in this life for Jesus. May the Lord bless you to move from one dimension of revelation of being multipliers to a greater dimension of revelation and practice of multiplying so that all the world may hear the great news of the gospel of Jesus Christ. For then, the fear of the LORD is alive and burning within our hearts to live this life in total abandon and surrender to God leading souls to Jesus and loving all those we encounter. Your life is ripe for the planting of the Word of the Lord so that a fruitful harvest may abound because of your abiding. Abiding yields wisdom, understanding, and direction, and the fear of the LORD is the beginning of wisdom.

> "For we are God's fellow workers; you are God's field, you *are* God's building" (1 Cor 3:9).

6

THE FEAR OF THE LORD
WHAT'S MISSING IN THE CHURCH?

"Therefore, since we are receiving a kingdom which cannot be shaken, let us have grace, by which we may serve God acceptably with reverence and godly fear. For our God is a consuming fire."

—Hebrews 12:28-29

All my life, I've had the privilege of growing up in the church. I'm so grateful to have been raised in a family who loves the Lord and saw the value of regularly attending church every week. I can recall going to Sunday morning church service as far back as I can remember. I can remember the sights, sounds, and even the smells of what church was like growing up. Admittedly, my favorite senses when I was a child involved smell and taste—yes, the wonderful sensation of delicious fresh-baked donuts waiting as my reward after an hour-long service. As a young child, those donuts were like striking gold after sitting through Church service. I must confess that much thought was put into looking forward to those donuts after service, which, in fact, was a major distraction for me from what Church was really supposed to be about.

Even as adults, in Church, there are still many of those distractions that capture our attention or even our affection, sometimes unknowingly. Our minds run busy through what took place throughout the week, what we accomplished or what we still need to get to. The endless to-do lists run through our minds and occupy valuable real estate in our thoughts, which become significant distractions to us, distractions that take us away from the presence of God. This busyness of the mind and the hustle and bustle of life have become a snare to Christians around the world, especially in Western culture. Much like children waiting for donuts, we can't wait to get to the end of service so we can get to our busy lives and to-do lists. But what's missing here?

There is something that is missing from the Church at large across the globe. Of course, I'm not making a blanket statement for *every* church, but I'm insinuating that the Church at large has a massive gap in our understanding and value of gathering corporately together around the presence of the Lord. I believe that at the core, what's missing is the fear of the LORD. At large, our lives have become busy, distracted, disconnected, and distant. I've had the blessing to visit many churches, and what I've seen in many places is this same crucial missing gap of the lack of fear of the Lord. I do not write this to present that I have 'arrived' and have a perfect understanding of the fear of the Lord. Rather, I desire to call attention to this desperate gap in relation to abiding that should bring awareness to each of our hearts. The hope is that, in sonship, we would then go to the Holy Spirit and have Him search our hearts and show us any way we have wandered away from the fear of the Lord or have neglected to value and appreciate God's presence in a way and lifestyle that brings Him the utmost honor.

> "You will show me the path of life; In Your presence *is* fullness of joy; At Your right hand *are* pleasures forevermore" (Ps 16:11).

If we were to honestly take inventory with the Holy Spirit and have Him search our hearts regarding how we have or have not walked in the fear of the Lord, what would we discover? What I've seen in my life in the past, and in the lives of many, is a casual, lukewarm, distracted, indifferent attitude to the presence of God. Perhaps worship is going on and we are carrying on a casual conversation. Or possibly we are caught up in how good or poor the music sounds and we are not connecting intimately to the Lord. Or maybe during communion, we have an offense in our hearts towards someone that is unresolved. During a service, perhaps our church has all the bells and whistles with the fanciest cameras, sound equipment, lights, smoke machines, and the best musicians, yet without the presence of Jesus, we have nothing. It is in His presence where we have the fullness of joy. There is nothing wrong with having this wonderful equipment to bring glory to Jesus, so long as it does not capture the affection of our hearts and distract the attention of our minds away from the Lord. I believe that this appreciation and reverence for Jesus in our lives and our churches is missing or lacking. But what exactly is the fear of the Lord?

What Is The Fear of the LORD?

Entire books have been written on the fear of the Lord. The heartbeat of this chapter aims to deepen our understanding of the fear of the Lord, as we aim to continually live our lives intimately abiding in and with the Lord. The fear of the Lord anchors us in walking out a life that is fully surrendered and obedient to the voice and direction of the Lord.

> "Let all the earth fear the Lord; Let all the inhabitants of the world stand in awe of Him" (Ps 33:8).

In the most basic understanding, the fear of the Lord is the holy awe and reverence of Almighty God. It is the heart's position of complete respect, humility, reverence, and honor for the Lord and His lordship over everything. It is not to be scared of God or to be confused with the same word of fear in the English language as we know it. That type of fear is the spirit of fear, which would drive away intimacy and create a dysfunctional relationship that creates greater distance rather than increasing closeness. No, rather, this fear of the Lord is the revelation of God's holiness, His power, His love, and unmatched greatness! It is the complete wonder of who Jesus is and the absolute praise, worship, and adoration of God alive in our hearts and flowing through our lives. This holy fear of God leads to greater, deepening intimacy with the Lord and attunement with His heart of perfect love. The awe of God ablaze in our hearts leads to overwhelming benefits that God promises us in His Word, which will result from the one who fears the Lord.

> "The fear of the Lord *leads* to life, And *he who has it* will abide in satisfaction; He will not be visited with evil" (Prov 19:23).

The Joy of The Fear of the LORD

Throughout the Word of God, there are over forty unique promises of blessings granted by God to the one who fears the Lord. All throughout Scripture, we read of men and women of God who embraced the fear of the Lord, as well as ones who didn't. Those who did fear the Lord were followed by the blessings of God throughout their lives. God's incredible promises to those who fear Him encompass various blessings: the key to deeper intimacy with Him, the beginning of wisdom, understanding, and knowledge; increased foresight and clear guidance; true and authentic holiness; bolstered confidence, fearlessness, and security; overcoming all other fears, like fear of man or failure; shaping our identity; fostering productivity and fruitful days; empowers multiplication; and releases great enjoyment in life! These are just some of the incredible blessings our loving Heavenly Father bestows upon those who love Him and obey Him out of holy fear.

> "Oh, fear the Lord, you his saints, for those who fear him have no lack" (Ps 34:9 ESV)!

Wow, just imagine for a minute what your life would look like with an increase in the holy fear of God! Perhaps you're just now discovering a glimpse of what the fear of the Lord is, or maybe you're living with a great awareness of the holy awe of God, which guides all your decisions. Possibly you find your life somewhere in between these two extremes. The great news is that no matter where you are along the spectrum, there is infinitely *more* to uncover! Yes, since God is immeasurable and infinite, there is infinitely more of Him to discover, and that means there is infinitely more of Him to be in holy awe of.

As you embrace this holy fear of the Lord, either for the first time or even more so in your life, an ever-increasing flow of God's promises will be unlocked in your life! The greatest joy of embracing God's awe is not even in the blessings that He releases into our lives. The greatest joy is in knowing Him. Knowing Him more and more and more every day in the upward-increasing journey of walking in greater intimacy in and with Him found in the holy fear of Him. This is essential in our lives of growing in becoming more firmly rooted in sonship and living out of the abiding.

"Teach me Your way, O Lord; I will walk in Your truth; Unite my heart to fear Your name" (Ps 86:11).

Sonship and The Fear of the LORD

"His mercy *is* on those who fear Him from generation to generation" (Luke 1:50).

I can remember many times in life when I had ignored the voice of the Holy Spirit and went with what I felt was best or with what I wanted and desired in my flesh. I can also attest that each of these times did not end well, to say the least! After giving my life fully over to Jesus, I began to gradually grow in the fear of the Lord. Although I did not have the language of what it was, I began growing in pure obedience to the voice of the Lord in my life. As my intimacy with Him continued to grow, my desire and appetite to follow the leading of the Holy Spirit rapidly grew. I had realized at that point in my life that everything good that had ever happened in my life was directly connected to the Lord.

I saw more and more of God's intimate affection in the smallest and largest of ways, both in my past and in the present. I would be undone by how intimately and intricately God knows me, even better than I know myself, and how He would tenderly communicate with me in the most incredible ways by knowing every detail of my heart and of the things that I love. Whether it was in seeing butterflies at just the right time, or in being overwhelmed by His presence sitting by a lake, every occurrence was drenched in perfect love that directly stemmed from the holy fear of the Lord alive in my heart.

I will never forget one of these times when the Lord blessed my sweet wife and me during our wedding planning. We had prayed together and sought God's will in all the planning, and He did not cease to amaze us! One evening in prayer, we sought the Lord for where we were to have our wedding ceremony, which was just eight months away. I was given a vision from the Lord of a beautiful wedding venue with huge white pillars at the front of the building. Later, when we were searching through wedding venues online, much to my amazement, I saw those same white pillars as I'd seen in my vision. We felt led to see about calling and scheduling a viewing time to check it out. After a few days had passed, my wife-to-be asked me if I'd called the venue yet. Having been busy, remembering to call them had slipped my mind for a few days. I called them the following day, and they asked for our wedding date. The staff said that the date I gave was available and that we could come to tour the venue that Sunday.

Once we arrived, the venue director informed us they were normally completely booked Thursday-Sunday an entire year in advance. He showed us their penciled-in calendar and said that our date was originally booked, but that was a few days prior. The couple had canceled their date and rescheduled a year later. To our amazement, and the director's, I had called just two days later requesting that very date which was now available! If that wasn't amazing enough, the date the Lord gave us for our wedding fell on a Thursday when the price was significantly less. Thank You, Jesus! We were amazed by the Lord and His perfect, unmatched ability to work all things together for our good as we remain submitted to His will, His way, and His timing. We had a glorious wedding ceremony and celebration of our covenant where souls were added to the Lamb's Book of Life, and a person was even healed physically in the presence of the Lord! Praise and glory to God!!

> "Blessed *is* the man *who* fears the Lord, *Who* delights greatly in His commandments" (Ps 112:1).

One of the greatest men of God whom I wholeheartedly respect and who has taught me about the holy fear of the Lord is John Bevere. John once made this statement that I feel perfectly connects the fear of the Lord with sonship, saying, "Obedience is the outward evidence of the fear of the Lord." This statement fully captures the heart of the person who is rooted in sonship and fears the Lord because the direct correlation of pure evidence is found in his or her *obedience* to God.

To embrace the fear of the Lord and live anchored in sonship is to have the ever-consistent evidence of our total obedience to God's voice and direction in our lives. We see some of the most radical examples of sonship and the fear of the Lord in the Bible with leaders such as Abraham when he left the land he knew and laid down his son Isaac, Gideon in the winepress, Moses before Pharaoh, and in the New Testament Matthew the tax collector who walked faithfully with Jesus, Peter who was a primary leader in the early Church or the terrorist Saul who became the apostle Paul. What I love is that in all these examples and so many more, none of these people were perfect. All had shortcomings and made mistakes, some even big mistakes. Yet also in the lives of all these heroes of faith, there is evidence found that they finished their races well and lived with the fear of the Lord that guided them as they worked out their salvation with holy fear and trembling.

"The holy fear of the Lord alive in one's life will never be void of pure, raw obedience to God." [1]

— JOHN BEVERE

Sonship anchored in the fear of the Lord releases the revelation and realization of God's perfect love, true security, protection, provision, affirmation, and overall purpose in this life, to name a few. It is the place of finding our true home, which is primarily and ultimately in Father God's loving embrace. From this place of our true home, we find the incredible exchange of intimate friendship with God which guards us from falling away from the faith or into legalism that's void of mercy and love.

> "By humility *and* the fear of the Lord *are* riches and honor and life" (Prov 22:4).

Living rooted in sonship with the fear of the Lord inside your heart unlocks the purpose of your existence and is the foundation of all happiness in life. Fearing God allows Him to be the one on the throne and for our flesh and self-guided efforts to take the back seat in life. It is the displacement of selfish ambition and self-seeking glory that's replaced with the burning passion of yielding everything to God and bringing Him all the glory of this life. Living with the awe of God alive in your heart releases His blessings of good health, productivity, success, elimination of lack, safety, and covering over you and all your household. These are just *some* joys of living with the life ambition and pure evidence through the obedience of one who fears the Lord! The holy fear of the Lord alive in one's life will never be void of pure, raw obedience to God.

> "Blessed is the one who fears the Lord always, but whoever hardens his heart will fall into calamity" (Prov 28:14 ESV).

It is in an instant with absolute obedience and no delay to God's voice that evidences a life flowing with the fear of the Lord. This sonship modeled through obedience is not dependent upon convenience, and when everything makes sense so one can see clearly the road that lies ahead. No, rather, it is the opposite, where much of the time, God is calling us out into the uncharted waters to "walk with Him on water" where we've not done so before and perhaps have seen no one else do so before. This is the beauty of a life completely yielded to Jesus that is rooted in sonship.

> "The fear of the Lord *is* the beginning of wisdom; A good understanding have all those who do *His commandments*. His praise endures forever" (Ps 111:10).

This raw obedience to God when we can't see the path, know the way, or understand the why and how of everything is where we exchange our logic for His Lordship. It is the place of laying everything we know down at the altar and surrendering to Him in complete trust, knowing that He is a good, holy, righteous Father who will never lead us astray, nor will He lead us to where we will sink in life. Having the utmost reverence, honor, respect, and wonder for God alive in our hearts will produce a garden within our lives that is solely tended by the Lover of our souls. This entrustment of everything to Jesus while laying down everything we are and everything we have to Him is the place of a realized holy awe of God. In relation to abiding, it is fully living out John 15:4-5, realizing that apart from God, we can do nothing. Nothing that will produce any true fruit that will remain and stand the test of time.

> "Abide in Me, and I in you. As the branch cannot bear fruit of itself, unless it abides in the vine, neither can you, unless you abide in Me. I am the vine, you *are* the branches. He who abides in Me, and I in him, bears much fruit; for without Me you can do nothing" (John 15:4-5).

I love this Scripture passage so much because God reveals to us in love that every pursuit that we seek on our own ability and ambitions will be void of producing any fruit for His Kingdom. In His perfect love, God is clearly telling us that *unless* we abide in Him and Him in us, we will never achieve the results we're seeking to achieve. Even the noblest of efforts that attempt to do good for humanity will not produce true fruit that will remain through the tides of time (John 15:16). God is fathering us through Jesus' words of pure truth in teaching us about what oneness looks like through abiding in and with Jesus. It is only in abiding in Him and with Him that we will truly understand His heart, know His ways, pray His will and tap into His endless wisdom. We will find the place of abiding, belonging, and resting in Jesus, and out of that will flow fruitfulness for His glory. As we seek to know Him more and follow His ways, we position His Lordship over everything in our lives, which opens us up for life-changing encounters with Him that will leave us forever marked.

Encountering God In The Unknown

There have been many times in life that the Lord has called my wife and me out into the uncharted waters. We could not see the shoreline or the path leading us to where we were going. At these times in life, we simply could not trust in our own ability, our logic, what seemed 'responsible,' or even what other godly people's voices were telling us. During these seasons of life, all we could hang onto was the Lord, embracing Jesus and trusting in Him with everything. Was it scary? Did we fear the unknown? Did the questions of 'what if' enter our minds? Perhaps. However, what was the most incredible and overwhelming part of these experiences was the sensation of total freedom found through the fear of the Lord. It was like the feeling of being on a sailboat, leaning forward on the bow of the ship, letting go of the ropes, and allowing the wind to hold you up as your arms are stretched out in total worship and surrender. These were the times in our lives when we felt the freest as we let go of the ropes of life and untethered away from any trust that was built on or placed in man, money, or anything else.

> "In the fear of the Lord *there* is strong confidence, And His children will have a place of refuge" (Prov 14:26).

I distinctly remember one of these times when the Lord was calling us out into the waters of the unknown. It was the season before He called us to plant the church that He called us to pastor and steward for His glory. Shortly after our second child was born, Jesus called for us to lay everything down afresh. God called for my wife to leave her workplace of 11 years and 11 months, and for us to leave nearly 90% of our income. God called us to sell our home, yet we didn't have a place to go. Our home sold after being listed for three days, and we dreamed with God about where He was calling us. We had our own ideas and dreams about where that would be. We dreamed of a beautiful home in the mountains with lots of land and beautiful scenery. However, it was in the abiding that we discovered God's heart and His plans for our lives. We surrendered wholeheartedly and laid down our personal desires and dreams that were contrary to what His dream was for us. We experienced an even closer intimacy with the Lord as He revealed bits and pieces of His dream for our lives. Still, we continued to 'walk on water' with Jesus as Abba Father pruned away what did not belong to the new season of fruitfulness ahead. It was in this very place that we encountered the heart of the Father unlike we'd ever known.

We embraced the fear of the Lord, which guided our hearts to HIS true north and not towards our fleshly desires and ambitions. It was through abiding with Him that the Holy Spirit revealed things we didn't even know we had that needed to be laid down in order to enter the new season ahead. As things were highlighted, we never felt shame or condemnation. We felt God's perfect love and total covering as He led us through that wilderness time. We simply embraced the pruning. Was it difficult and challenging? Yes, absolutely it was, but it was more beautiful than there are words to describe. We were overwhelmed by the nearness of God's presence and how tender loving His heart is for every one of us.

"Sometimes fruitfulness has to grow in one season before it's seen in the next." [2]

— NICHOLAS BARTA

In this place of exchange, we discovered more of what God had for us. As time went on, we saw more of the complete picture and experienced what the Lord had intended for us. Sometimes, fruitfulness has to grow in one season before it's seen in the next. That's how our story went! After the Lord moved us into where He had planned for us to live for the next season, the unexpected came. The entire world went into lockdown as COVID broke out across the world. But God is Lord over every season! Even as everything was practically locked down, God was opening things up. In a season and time when churches and places were closing their doors, God was planting and opening His church! We got to see the miracle of provision from the Lord carry us through the past season when the numbers did not add up, yet He still sent checks and surprises in the mail to provide for our family. We got to see a greater realization of Isaiah 55:8-9, which says:

> "For My thoughts *are* not your thoughts, Nor *are* your ways My ways," says the Lord. For *as* the heavens are higher than the earth,

So are My ways higher than your ways, And My thoughts than your thoughts" (Isa 55:8-9).

As we learn to yield over all of our understanding, wisdom, logic, and reasoning to the Lord, He remains ever faithful to outdo and overwhelm us with His ways and His will that are always higher and more incredible than we could ever imagine. Embracing the fear of the Lord and choosing to follow His leading no matter how it looks or what people say will position you to encounter God in life-changing ways. In that season of our life, when we laid everything down by His grace, we saw the hand of God provide, protect, cover, and release blessings unlike we ever had before. What was the best part of it all? Greater intimacy with Him! There is no measure nor words to articulate how wonderful the life of abounding in fruitful intimacy with the Lord is. He is our all who fills us. Increased intimacy with God pays dividends into eternity!

In all my ability to do anything in life, anything worthy of bearing any fruit for God, I fully recognize that it is ALL by His grace. Apart from the vine, a branch cannot produce any fruit. Even as you read this testimony from our lives, it was still completely by God's grace that we could surrender, and by His grace, we partnered with the Holy Spirit to plant a work for the Lord. In listening to His voice that was leading and guiding us, it was the fear of the Lord in our hearts that activated us to say yes to His invitation. The holy fear of the Lord in our hearts created an alignment that was necessary to cross the unknown waters into the new territory He was calling us into. It was our alignment with God's heart and His will that came before He released His assignment for us in the new land.

Kingdom Alignment BEFORE Kingdom Assignment

As we deepen our understanding and increase our hunger for the spirit of the fear of the Lord, we will find ourselves in a position of being brought into alignment with God's will and plan for our lives. For me, I don't want to be on the general board or vicinity of His plan for my life. No, I desire to be in the absolute center of His will and plan for my life. I believe that this is you too! The central way to achieve that ambition is to fear the Lord with every decision we make. My wife and I are certainly in process and continually growing in this, but thanks to God, we're not where we started by far!

As you hunger for and cry out to God for the holy fear and awe of Him, He will grace you with the ability to reverence Him and give Him the utmost position of authority and Lordship over every part of your life. Perhaps you're strong in following His voice in every area until it involves money. Or maybe you're strong in following His direction until it involves sacrifice. Or perhaps you're solid in every area of your life until it involves laying down your family. Whatever and wherever God wants to grow you, it will always come with the fruit of obedience rooted in sonship through the holy fear of God evidenced in your life.

"Kingdom alignment will always precede Kingdom assignment." [3]

— LEIF HETLAND

The encouragement here is that all of us can and should grow in the fear of the Lord, and to do so continually throughout our lives! There will always be an area in the changing seasons of life where we can grow in this virtue by His grace, and we will be brought into greater alignment with God's plan and purposes that will eventually produce greater fruit in the season ahead. This fruit will only come as we abide in the true vine, Jesus Christ, and remain in life-union with Him. As we do this, we are brought into alignment with God where Father God lovingly tends to the parts of us that need pruning.

As we learn from the lifestyle of abiding in oneness with the Lord, Jesus teaches us in John 15 that Father God will even prune that which bears fruit so that it may bear even greater fruit and fruit that will remain. Pruning is simply a part of the Kingdom life, and it is the pre-requisite to discovering our Kingdom assignment in Him. Kingdom alignment will always precede Kingdom assignment. In finding this alignment within our hearts to not only love the Lord with all of our heart, soul, mind, and strength but also to have the holy fear of Him evidenced through our decisions, we find that the Holy Spirit will bring greater influence, blessing, and increase because of our obedience to follow Him. Yet, in order to discover more of our Kingdom assignment in life, let's first go even deeper with what the fruit of obedience looks like through a surrendered life that is abiding in Jesus.

> "The friendship of the Lord is for those who fear him, and he makes known to them his covenant" (Ps 25:14 ESV).

> "The end of the matter; all has been heard. Fear God and keep his commandments, for this is the whole duty of man" (Eccl 12:13 ESV).

7

OBEDIENT LOVE
TRUST IN HIM

I've heard it said that trust is built upon the exchange of truth. We can and will be more apt to cultivate deeper relationships with those with whom we share life experiences. The depth of a relationship can be measured by the length at which those people exchange vulnerability, transparency, humility, and truth. Where these four ingredients flourish in a relationship, there will be solid evidence of a close, heart-to-heart connection that can last a lifetime.

I love the stories of people who are in their 70s and 80s who have had their closest friends with them since grade school. You just can't put a price tag on how valuable that truly is! Imagine the stories that could be shared and the life wisdom that could be drawn on from people like this. I believe that if you were to sit and have a cup of coffee with them, a great wealth of wisdom would be shared not just from the cherished fun memories together, but also from the hardships they've walked through with each other. These hardships, when walked fully through, can produce a deepened level of trust and closeness that would have otherwise not been there had they not walked through it *together*.

You see, our history with God is the most valuable treasure in this life. Day by day, we get the privilege and blessing to cultivate a closer, deeper connection with the Lord as we uncover more of His glorious heart of perfect love. Yet if we have points of pain and hardship in life where we did not get the answer as to why something happened or why we lost our loved one, these very places will create a block in our hearts, preventing us from being able to fully receive from God and to fully give Him our complete, undivided trust.

We will obey the one in whom we have placed our trust. However, if there are areas of pain from disappointment, loss, difficulty, and hardship that have not been resolved, we will have open doors for pain to rule and closed doors to love operating. I believe that this is so key because it unveils what's really in our hearts and gives us the ability to seek the Lord tenderly where we have some of these areas in our hearts that are preventing us from trusting in Him in walking into the unknown. These are the opportunities for the greatest breakthrough to come into our lives to bring about a greater trust and deeper relationship with the Lord that releases an increased hunger and desire to obey Him in whatever He calls us to. Opening our hearts to Him in these places of pain can and will bring about healing, freedom, and newness of life. As we learned in chapter two, He is the gentle heart gardener who will gently tend to our heart garden and bring about restoration and healing as we trust in Him.

Our level of trust in the Lord will determine our willingness to follow and obey Him. Our aim in living the abiding lifestyle is to ensure that no place of our hearts is closed off to Jesus but to allow the Holy Spirit an absolute all-access pass to all our hearts so that we may continually flourish in our relationship with Him. I believe that this is what David was crying out to God when He wrote in the Psalms,

> "Search me, God, and know my heart; test me and know my anxious thoughts. See if there is any offensive way in me, and lead me in the way everlasting" (Ps 139:23-24 NIV).

This is the heart's cry of sonship! As we continue to work out our salvation day by day and moment by moment, only He can reveal to us the ways that have prohibited and prevented us from receiving His love and walking in a close relationship built upon total trust in Him. Our God has never faulted or errored in any way—He is perfect in every way, and all His ways are good (Ps 145:17). The position of sonship is to recognize that we are to never lift our experiences and limited understanding above His Lordship. When we have the opportunities in life to trust in Him when we cannot see and when we do not understand, our lives abound with significant growth and fruitfulness in our intimate relationship with the Lord.

I think of the life of Abraham, who, after waiting twenty-five years for the 'impossible' promise of God to manifest with his son Isaac being miraculously conceived and born. What an incredible story of trust, trial, and promise realized! Just think of the faith it took to believe in God for what was completely impossible in the natural with bearing a child at such an old age. In addition to this, look at God's incredible mercy in fulfilling His promise even after Abram and Sarai faltered when the maidservant Hagar conceived and gave birth to Ishmael (see Gen 16). What's perhaps even more amazing is that even after this long-awaited promise of Isaac came and much life and joy was shared as a family, God spoke and called Abraham to do the unimaginable. God called Abraham to lay it all down.

Genesis 22:1-19 captures this incredible journey of radical obedience to one who loved the Lord and had a holy fear of God that led to unmatched obedience to His voice. Genesis 22:2 says,

> "Then He said, 'Take now your son, your only *son* Isaac, whom you love, and go to the land of Moriah, and offer him there as a burnt offering on one of the mountains of which I shall tell you'" (Gen 22:2).

There was no doubting what God had spoken to Abraham. It was clear and concise: lay it all down. In the next verse, we read Abraham responded immediately in obedience to the voice of the Lord. It says that Abraham rose early in the morning and made all the preparations necessary, including splitting the wood for the burnt offering. That is radical obedience without delay, questioning, or doubting. God spoke, Abraham moved. He moved because he feared the Lord and trusted in His goodness. We see in verse five of Abraham's deep level of trust in the Lord as he said, "Stay here with the donkey; the lad and I will go yonder and worship, and we will come back to you." How could Abraham say that if He knew God had called Him to lay down his promised son Isaac as an offering to the Lord? Here, Abraham showed complete trust and total faith in the Lord, yet it did not stop there.

In verse ten, we read Abraham lifting the knife to slay his son and following through with the directive of the Lord. Being interrupted by the Angel of the Lord, Abraham stops and declares his wholehearted devotion to the Lord as he states, "Here I am." Then the Angel unveils the test of the Lord as He said in verse twelve,

> "And He said, 'Do not lay your hand on the lad, or do anything to him; for now I know that you **fear God**, since you have not withheld your son, your only *son*, from Me'" (*bold added for emphasis* Gen 22:12).

Here, we see Abraham's test of faith, trust, devotion to the Lord, and his unwithheld fear of the Lord modeled through total obedience to His voice. Then we see the faithfulness of Father God in providing the ram caught in the thicket as the sacrifice for the burnt offering that He was requesting. Abraham then declared over the place "The-LORD-Will-Provide," Yahweh Yireh, and proclaimed an incredible prophetic declaration as he said, "In the Mount of the LORD it shall be provided" (Gen 22:14).

Because of His love for God and the holy fear of the Lord, Abraham went the complete distance of obedience built upon absolute trust in the Lord even when things seemed unimaginably difficult, with no answers given as to why he was to lay down the son of promise and sacrifice him. Can you even imagine the mental and emotional struggle that he possibly went through?? There must have been a surge of thoughts and ideas running through his mind. Although we are not given any specific details about this scripturally, we can certainly imagine a glimpse of what it must have been like. Yet one thing we see clearly, and that is, that Abraham did not waiver in his trust in the Lord and his obedience to His voice. As a reward of blessing, Father God blessed all the seeds of Abraham's inheritance that would ever walk the earth.

> "By Myself I have sworn, says the Lord, because you have done this thing, and have not withheld your son, your only *son*—blessing I will bless you, and multiplying I will multiply your descendants as the stars of the heaven and as the sand which *is* on the seashore; and your descendants shall possess the gate of their enemies. In your seed all the nations of the earth shall be blessed, because you have **obeyed** My voice" (*bold added for emphasis* Gen 22:16-18).

Abraham's incredible level of trust was built from his intimacy with God and his holy fear of the Lord, which guided the decisions of his life. No matter what any other voice, including his own thoughts, may have tried to say, Abraham attuned his heart and ears only to the voice of the LORD. Perhaps Abraham was never offered the 'why' behind why God had taken him on this test of faith and obedience. Maybe Abraham never knew the real depth of why God called him to lay down his only begotten son, Isaac, whom he waited, prayed for, and believed for so long.

It's likely that you, too, have scratched your head at the mystery of things in your past where you did not have the answers as to why. However, for us all here living on the other side of the cross, we have been blessed with God's revelation of His why behind Abraham's test of faith.

Scholars have discovered that the hills of Moriah, where God called Abraham to lay down his son Isaac, were the same hills as those in Jerusalem, where Jesus Christ was lifted on the cross in Golgotha. The same area where God encountered Abraham and Isaac was the same area where Father God laid down His only Son for the sake of all humanity. Although it couldn't yet be revealed what God was doing with Abraham, we now see that the Father was setting the stage for a prophetic foreshadowing of His Son Jesus, who would be offered as a living sacrifice for all mankind.

The cross, as we know, stands forever as our symbol of salvation, as we always remember the price Jesus paid in His radical, unmatched obedience to the Father's will of the pathway for the redemption of mankind. Obedient love at its finest is exemplified in the laid-down life of Jesus Christ, our Lord, Savior, and King. In the Bible, Philippians 2:8, it says,

> "And being found in appearance as a man, He humbled Himself and became obedient to *the point* of death, even the death of the cross" (Phil 2:8).

Trust is our exchange with God where we have given everything, all that we are, over to His Lordship in our lives. As we grow in a greater revelation of our abiding in oneness with Him, we will see greater fruit beyond anything we imagined. We are blessed to know the heights, depths, widths, and lengths of the love of God that leaves us continually forever marked and transformed. As you yield over even more of your heart and choose to trust God with even more unexplored areas of your heart, you will walk in a greater level of trust that produces greater unrestricted obedience to His voice as He leads you along the path of life.

> "Trust in the Lord with all your heart, And lean not on your own understanding; In all your ways acknowledge Him, And He shall direct your paths" (Prov 3:5-6).

Sometimes, we have to let go in order to learn how to hold on. Just as Abraham was richly blessed for his obedience to God, we too, are richly rewarded for every act of obedience through the love that we give unto Him. Yet, in order to walk in this, there is a cost of greater humility needed in and through our lives that unlocks our hearts from being bound by deception or by the misleading of our flesh.

Humble Hearts

When we are in seasons of tests given by the Lord, we often find ourselves in a weakened, more dependent state. Have you ever noticed that when you were walking through a challenging season, your ability to cling to the Lord was even closer? It's like yesterday's manna just won't satisfy, but you need today and every day, fresh daily bread of His presence. Jesus is our daily bread! Father God intends to grow and stretch us in these times of trial, testing, or even persecution. There is not one thing that God is not familiar with. Hebrews 4:15 says,

> "For we do not have a High Priest who cannot sympathize with our weaknesses, but was in all *points* tempted as *we are*, yet without sin" (Heb 4:15).

No matter what we face in life, we are assured that God is with us. He understands everything we are going through and will lead us through it all. In these times, a greater humility in our hearts is needed for His work to be done in us, which is necessary for us to cross over into the new land and spiritual territory He's calling us into.

As we learn more of what it means to 'trust in the Lord with *all* our hearts,' we realize that each day and every moment, we need Jesus and that we depend on His abiding presence to walk us through this life by His Holy Spirit in us. Our humility before Him is to acknowledge our weaknesses and inability to produce or do anything apart from Him. This is the life of living rooted in sonship, a life flowing with a continual awareness of our value to Him and our commissioning to labor with Him in all He calls us to do. Acknowledging our weaknesses and inabilities is not to think less of ourselves or to have a pity party. It is intended for us to realize to a greater degree that even in our greatest of times and strongest anointing, we can truly accomplish nothing without Him.

"Our humility before Him is to acknowledge our weaknesses and inability to produce or do anything apart from Him." [1]

— NICHOLAS BARTA

Intimately crying out to Father God through the Spirit of Adoption positions us to encounter Him and learn His ways so that we can follow His narrow path that leads to a life led by the Spirit and not by the flesh (see Rom 8:9-14). Every single one of us can and has been misled by our fleshly desires, thoughts, ideas, and ambitions, even well-meaning ones. I have found that humility of the heart kills selfish desires and positions us in the right alignment with God's will when we follow His redirecting us.

> "But He gives more grace. Therefore He says: 'God resists the proud, But gives grace to the humble.'" (Jas 4:6).

Our weaknesses and mistakes aren't to bring shame and condemnation to our hearts, but are to point us to our primary and ultimate need for more of Jesus! What a beautiful revelation to seize opportunities of failure, weakness, and inability and to view them as priceless times of encountering God's grace, leading us to grow in greater humility and dependence upon Him. The orphan led by the flesh will never be willing to admit fault or need, but the son led by the Spirit rejoices in growing in greater dependence upon the Lord, even if it is through chastening by God. As noted in the previous chapter, this is the realized place of John 15:4-5, which is that apart from Him, we can do nothing. Even when life and ministry flourish with fruitfulness, and you operate at greater levels of your strongest anointing, it is *still* by God's grace. Never rely on your own anointing. Embrace the Anointed One and let Him lead you beside the still waters of His glorious presence.

Our Position Is Submission

Living a life of increased growth in humility and dependence upon God will usher in an increased desire in you for total submission to Him. Just as we see how the life of Jesus modeled perfect sonship through total submission to the Father, we too, are called to live with our position as submission to Him in all things. Even when it makes little sense, when no answers are given, when you cannot hear His voice or that He's just not speaking, these are the valuable times in life to submit to Him with your all and follow His Spirit's leading as you wait upon the Lord.

Through sonship, God calls us to submit willingly to Him and His ways, plan, and timing, just as He did with His Son Jesus. God's loving invitation is warmly welcoming us to lay everything down into His loving hands. Psalm 55:22 says that you are to "Cast your burden on the LORD, And He shall sustain you; He shall never permit the righteous to be moved." Our loving Father promises us He will indeed take our burdens, especially the burden of having to figure everything out on our own. As we learn to submit our own desires and dreams to the Lord, He is faithful to sift through them lovingly, pruning and purifying that which is of Him in His perfect will for our lives. In surrendering to God's will and His ways for our life, we are forfeiting the pressures, hardship, and demands of having to figure everything out in our own ability. In exchange, we are positioning ourselves to be fathered by Him, which produces a loving exchange of intimate relationship and partnership with the Lord rather than the orphan-led independent spirit that strives and struggles on one's own.

For much of my life, I had lived that way, striving through life and trying to figure out things on my own. I made wrong turns, found dead ends, and got rerouted more times than I can count. Sometimes, in His perfect love, Father allowed me to go around a mountain more than once or twice so that I could see my genuine need for His leadership and fathering in my life. Perhaps you have had the same type of experience in your life? Maybe you are currently struggling with a decision to make or a thing to work through. Please take this advice to save much time and effort. Wholeheartedly submit your will, your desires, your perceived outcome, and the timing of everything, and let Abba father you. Yes, this submission and surrender costs you, but it is nothing compared to the cost of lost time and spent energy striving on your own. The only way for us to ensure our motives, plans and ambitions are from the Lord is to surrender them fully to God and allow Him to sift through them to bring about His will in our lives.

God instructs us in His Word to make plans, but it is He who will establish our steps (Proverbs 16:9). Those plans that we are to make are not intended to be apart from Him, but flowing in oneness with Him. All His ways are good, and He will work out everything for our good according to His plan (Rom 8:28). Our job in this place of sonship submission to Him is to increase our dependence upon Him in every area, even the ones that feel scary and challenging for us to let go of.

Dependence Upon The Rock

As Christians, our true, solid foundation is solely and primarily founded upon the Rock of our salvation, Jesus Christ. So naturally, everything we aim to build in this life should be built upon that solid foundation, for it is the only *true* foundation that will stand the test of time and trial. However, as I mentioned earlier in this chapter, it seems far too common and too easy for us to slip into dependence on our own strengths, abilities, or anointing. The life of abiding will come with the cost of the forfeiture of these misguided trusts and place us in a position that feels perhaps uncomfortable and uncertain. These are the places where the Holy Spirit draws us the same way He led Jesus into the wilderness right after He was publicly affirmed by His Father. It is in these places of the unknown that we must grow in dependence upon Jesus, even as He leads us to places where we're doomed if He doesn't show up.

I love these places where stories of real, raw, unrestricted faith in my heroes' lives are shared, where they share the glory of God showing up and Him showing off! It's so encouraging and invigorating to read stories like this that challenge and awaken us to an invitation to a surrendered life that is completely laid down and fully dependent upon the Lord to show up.

One of these stories I love is from my spiritual father, Papa Leif Hetland, who shared a time when he ministered in a nation in the Middle East. Leif and his team put up posters around the city of this big event they were hosting. On the posters, it stated that Jesus was going to be there, and that there was going to be healing. How awesome and bold is that? As the meeting took place, Jesus began to heal and touch people through Leif, ministering and preaching the gospel. However, not everyone loved this gospel news, and there was a group of radical Muslims who came with machine guns to eliminate the 'infidel' who had been falsely accused of supposedly speaking against their faith. As they rushed to the stage carrying their weapons in hand, the glory of God hit them, and they began dancing and rejoicing as God's love and joy filled their hearts for the first time!

Can you imagine what that must have been like? Picture this scene in your mind, and imagine what God's glory arresting these beloved men looked like. As amazing as this story is, it would not have come about had it not been for Papa Leif's total dependence on Jesus to come to this meeting. As God's beloved son, Leif heard from the Father to host this healing festival, print the flyers, hang them around town, and spread the news of this event. Leif completely depended upon the Lord to show up, putting himself in a very uncomfortable position out of his raw obedience to the Lord. The result? God showed up big time! There was an outbreak of miracles and salvations, leaving this region and nation forever impacted by the glory of God! Now, that's what total dependence and raw obedience can do for the glory of King Jesus!

"Full dependence that God will lead you, opens you to see the path He's called you to follow." [2]

— NICHOLAS BARTA

Although most of us may not have wild and incredible stories like Papa Leif's sharing, make no mistake, your obedience to God, even in the smallest of details, is of no less value. Every act of obedience to the Lord is greatly celebrated, and all is necessary for the building blocks that build up to the larger things He calls you to. This growth of dependence upon the Lord will trade your confidence for 'God-fidence,' your reasoning for His wisdom, and your logic for His Lordship. Your ability to acknowledge your deep, continual need for Jesus in all things will always unlock greater blessings, favor, and increase in ways you may have never suspected. As you determine in your heart to know that you cannot and will not move forward on your own ability, strength, gifts, or intellect, you will find an increased experience of God's manifest presence. May we find our lives just like Moses when he said, "If You don't come with us, we will not go in (Ex 33:14-16)." As you cry out to the Lord with this same heart posture, you will position yourself in submission to all He calls you to do.

Often, this is required before hearing our next steps of direction that His voice of truth will speak in the wilderness times. Full dependence that God will lead you opens you to see the path He's called you to follow. We cannot see with our natural eyes what He's painted in the spirit for our spiritual eyes to see. Only those who are led by the Spirit of God will truly be called sons and daughters of God (Rom 8:14). Dependence on God to provide, guide, protect, grant wisdom, direct, and correct will position you to encounter the Lord of the supernatural. These encounters, like Leif's, will leave you forever marked by God, intending to increase an unquenchable hunger for more of Him that leaves you fully satisfied yet longing for more. As that more is released from His hand, the ever-deepening well of humility must continue to be dug, lower and lower still, so that the river of His presence and provision continues to flow.

Obedience through Opposition

When I think of the times in life when my obedience was the most expensive, it was when there was opposition or hardship attached to the decision to walk out onto the waters with Jesus. One of the more memorable times when this took place was on my first trip to the Middle East in a Muslim nation. During this trip, I had the privilege to preach and minister to hundreds of people as I watched God pour out His glory through hundreds of physical healing miracles and many salvations. On my second to last day there, we had coordinated to host a large healing crusade where close to 5,000 people would be present. The morning before our event was to take place later that evening, there was an uproar that broke out across the city and region. Some Christian pastors local in that same city were falsely accused of burning the Quran and blaspheming their god. What took place next was terrifying among the persecuted Christian community there.

Within a matter of a few brief hours, hundreds of Christian homes were burned, dozens of Christian churches were destroyed, and even a Christian graveyard was desecrated. The pastor who hosted me asked what I wanted to do: to flee or stay. As we remained in our hotel room near chaos, I felt the complete shalom peace of God had surrounded me. I had a strong sense that the Lord put on my heart that I was exactly where He wanted me to be in order to pray and intercede for what was taking place. Supernaturally, there was no fear present, but bold passion and power prayers rose collectively with sons and daughters all over the world who had heard the news of what was taking place in this nation. We prayed late into the night as the same pastors I was serving with were the heroes in the night, driving the Christian families to safety.

Once our prayer assignment was complete, the Lord led us to leave early that morning under the cover of night to get to the city that I needed to fly out of that next day. The Lord showed me that in our obedience to stay and to pray, He heard our prayers in Heaven and responded powerfully by preserving the lives of hundreds of Christians who were evacuated from the area. Not one life was lost, even though roughly 300 homes and 30 churches were burned and destroyed. Now, that's the power of our God in response to our obedience to His voice, even amid great tension, opposition, and trial! All glory be to King Jesus!!

There is a strength of trust formed and a deeper relationship cultivated with God when we trust in Him not only in the unknown, but in the heat of the opposition incurred when we follow His will and listen to His voice. I believe that these times of raw obedience to the Lord in the midst of persecution and opposition forge the release of unique blessings of increase by God into our lives, which will eventually bring about greater fruit for His glory. It is that very glory of God that we can uniquely experience in the heat of opposition that will form even greater character within us and more potent perseverance through our obedience to endure whatever is in front of us. The Lord teaches us in Romans 5:3-6,

> "And not only *that*, but we also glory in tribulations, knowing that tribulation produces perseverance; and perseverance, character; and character, hope. Now hope does not disappoint, because the love of God has been poured out in our hearts by the Holy Spirit who was given to us. For when we were still without strength, in due time Christ died for the ungodly" (Rom 5:3-6).

Here, we read of a man, Paul, who was well acquainted with suffering for the sake of the gospel. Paul learned to embrace the Lord with deep closeness amid the intense tribulations he faced, knowing that there was a glory that would be experienced. This was a glory far surpassing, incredible glory that far outweighs any minor, temporary suffering, hardship, and opposition that he endured. Even in the times that felt the most grueling, uncomfortable, and virtually unable to bear, he pressed in closer to Jesus through His extreme, unrelenting obedience to the Lord. Paul wrote about these times of pressing in his second letter to the Corinthians:

> "We are hard-pressed on every side, yet not crushed; we are perplexed, but not in despair; persecuted, but not forsaken; struck down, but not destroyed— always carrying about in the body the dying of the Lord Jesus, that the life of Jesus also may be manifested in our body" (2 Cor 4:8-10).

I love reading the epistles written by Paul through the Holy Spirit because they give us a renewed ambition to pursue Jesus with everything in our lives. These epistles inspire us to live completely laid down before the Lord in absolute obedience in sonship to anything and everything that He calls us to do. Even in the times that are the most pressing in this life, we are given such fresh bread from the holy Word of God that we will not be crushed, we will not be in despair, we will not be struck down, nor will we be destroyed. Yet, in the pressing process, the oil is formed. Yes, it is in the uncomfortable, challenging, squeezing times that we are formed more into the image of Christ. As we trust in Him and worship through our times of greatest challenge and opposition, we cultivate a rich oil through the pressing that becomes the oil of intimacy that fills our lamps. Even though we are promised by Jesus that we will endure tribulations in this life, we are assured that Jesus has overcome the world and everything in it (John 16:33).

"In the process of the pressing is where the oil is formed." [3]

— NICHOLAS BARTA

It is in these very times that we, just like the apostle Paul, can experience the glory of and from the Lord that draws us into a deeper place of intimacy and friendship with God that lasts for eternity. In these times, we are to remember that we are always "carrying about in the body the dying of the Lord Jesus" to remind us that our flesh is crucified with Christ. We cannot be fruitful through the works of the flesh, nor will the leadership of our flesh lead us into the will of God. But it is through "the life of Jesus that is manifested in our body" that will bring us into the glory of the resurrection life of Jesus Christ, alive IN us!

The awareness of Christ's resurrection life alive inside us leads to the glory of revelation of the Son of God that will enable us and carry us through the storms and trials of this life. The resurrection power of Him living in us will bring about His glory through us. It is in this revelation of God's glory that we can glory in tribulations because we know that the goodness and great love of God will work all things together for our ultimate good and, while doing so, form us more into the image of Christ. As we are continually formed more and more into His image and likeness, we become closer and closer to His heart of perfect love, which leads to a friendship with God that grows and flourishes as we remain abiding in Him.

Worship Music to Encounter Him [4]

8

A FRIEND OF GOD

INFINITE ACCESS AND FULLNESS

I used to think as a young man that becoming a friend of God was something that was far out of my reach and that it was virtually unattainable. My thinking was that only the very select few, the 'elite' Christians, could reach the status of becoming a 'friend of God.' I thought God would only value me for what I could do for Him, and I just needed to always obey Him. As we've covered already, obedience is absolutely essential, and it flows out of the love that we have for the Lord. But at this time in my life, I thought that obedience was to always be a servant who is faithful unto my Master, and that's what defines the confines of our relationship.

While I was working in the garage, I had an encounter with the Lord. I will never forget this encounter when He spoke to me and told me I was truly His friend. I was absolutely wrecked by His kindness and loving intimacy extended toward me. I found myself having a hard time trying to grasp and believe it. Before any doubt could enter my mind, my sweet wife leaned into the garage, having just heard from the Holy Spirit, and said, "Babe, you truly are a friend of God!" Neither one of us had discussed this topic of being a friend of God any time recently, yet in His perfect ability, God spoke this revelation to my heart and simultaneously to my wife, laying it on her heart to stop what she was doing and come share it with me. If that were not amazing enough, shortly after that, the Holy Spirit then put on my worship playlist, a song about being a friend of God. I was so touched by His loving invitation and declaration that I fell on my face in worship on that dirty garage floor, amazed by the love of our Heavenly Father!

At that season in my life, I understood God looks at the heart of man and that He sees all that He's placed in each one of us. Father God was not measuring our relationship based on what I could do for Him or my flawless ability to follow His voice and His ways. God was calling out to me, seeing my heart pursuing Him and His ways, and I was operating in friendship with Him. In just a moment's time, He broke the mindset I once had that being a friend of God was reserved for only the top elite Christians. How ridiculous that sounds! God showed me that His heart and will for friendship with His sons and daughters is available to all those who seek His face, hunger to know Him, long to discover His heart, and follow His ways. As we abide in His presence, we come more in tune with His heart so that we can know Him more and follow His ways. When we are shining with His presence, we see that glorious oneness manifested through us that reaches out unto Him and creates an inseparable bond of loving friendship. We see Jesus' very heart in John 15:15, where he says,

> "No longer do I call you servants, for a servant does not know what his master is doing; but I have called you friends, for all things that I heard from My Father I have made known to you" (John 15:15).

Here, we see clearly that Jesus' heart is an intimate relationship through a close friendship with Him that will last into eternity. We see Jesus' invitation to that place of access into His heart to know what is most important to Him, as revealed by the Father. Jesus warmly invites us to know His heart in such a close, intimate way so that we can come to understand the things that He desires to do. Jesus conveyed that there is absolutely nothing withheld from us as revealed to Him in His relationship with Father God as He spoke, *"for all things that I heard from My Father, I have made them known to you."* Isn't it incredible to think that Jesus has made known to us, and will make known to us that which is from our

Heavenly Father? He has withheld nothing back from the intimacy and closeness that He shares with Abba Father and has extended that towards all who remain abiding with Him in intimate relationship. The Lord gives us that same place of access to the heart of God.

"There isn't a closer, more intimate invitation than oneness." [1]

— NICHOLAS BARTA

It is so wild to me to think that the God who created everything, all the world, all the animals, all of humanity, and the entire universe, would want to be in close intimate friendship with us as His children. I mean, have you ever thought about the depths of what that means to live out practically in our lives? Jesus longs to have such close friendship with us, as it says in the Scriptures that there is a friend who sticks closer than a brother (Proverbs 18:24). God holds us up strong in His love so that we will never be left alone, sidelined, disregarded, or labeled as unimportant because He is with us and in us, and He always desires to have close intimate friendship with all those longing to know His heart.

One of the most beautiful revelations of friendship with God found in this verse in John 15 is that the Lord extends this warm invitation of close friendship that is found only through abiding in Him. There isn't a closer, more intimate invitation than oneness. This oneness, through abiding, is the context of what Jesus spoke in John 15:15. The confines of this invitation have no bounds, no ending, no expiration date, nor can it possibly be measured because He is endless, and His heart of perfect love is endless for us. As we abide in Him and He abides in us, we discover more and more of His heart that is made known to us through intimacy. Remaining in abiding in and with the Lord will open up the realm of infinite access and fullness of relational oneness through close friendship with God.

Since the Lord is infinite, the ability to discover more and more of His heart is truly endless! Jesus's invitation to friendship with God extends over 2000 years to each of us here today. His heart is that you would be so close that you would not only hear His heartbeat and know His ways, but that your heart would beat in sync with His. We become friends with God when we have learned as sons and daughters to serve Him faithfully, obey Him always, and learn ever-increasingly how we have total access to His heart.

Father God looks at us through the lens of His Son's Blood, which has made us clean, righteous, and holy before Him in love (Col 1:19-22). Because of the Blood of Jesus, every born-again believer in Jesus Christ has absolute access to the infinite fullness of God, to discover not only here on Earth but also for all eternity. I believe that when we get to heaven, and we stand before God face to face in glory, for all eternity, we will discover new sides of His holy face and endless facets of His heart as we abide in eternal oneness together with the Father, the Son, and the Holy Spirit.

Jesus's invitation into friendship with God is made completely available by His Blood to each one of us today. God's heart is that we would come to know that we can come to Him as we would come to our closest friend, tell Him anything that is on our mind, and share anything that is weighing on our hearts. This very lifestyle of the exchange of the most intimate parts of our hearts being vulnerably shared is what true friendship is all about. This exchange of life always and ultimately flows between us. The Lord is first so that we know how to receive love and then give love to our neighbor. Those who are rooted and grounded in love know how to guard and steward what their closest friends share from their hearts. This exchange of close, intimate friendship becomes a treasure so great that no price tag could ever be allotted to it.

Becoming more fully immersed and deeply rooted in sonship will flourish as we grow not only our ability to share the things most intimate to our hearts, but also learn to listen and discover what is most intimate to our Father's heart. As sons and daughters of God, we continue to grow in stewarding the revelations flowing from the heart of God into our hearts. We see a significant transformation in our lives, in the lives surrounding us, and even within the microcultures that we find ourselves in. As we learn more about God's heart through a close friendship with Him, we will also become more and more like Him, capable of thinking how He thinks and responding in the way He would. This perfect love flowing from our relationship with God will leaven every part of us with Himself. This love found only through abiding will bring a transformation to every part within us, leading to a continually growing intimacy and a flourishing friendship that our hearts deeply long for. Therefore, we must continually be led by Him to grow in Him and become more like Him.

Lovingly Led And Fed

With an ever-growing intimate friendship, all the direction and correction that we could ever need is already available through the Holy Spirit in us. The beauty of this truth is that we never need to rely on our own ability to fabricate the solution to the problems we face, to figure out what we're supposed to do or the direction we are to go. God has intended for us to commune with Him in intimate relationships and close friendships so that we can come to Him all the time with whatever we need. This is one of the core attributes of becoming more firmly rooted in sonship. It is the ability to lay down all of our own capability, and wholeheartedly and willingly be led by the Lord.

Romans 8:14 says, *"For as many as are led by the Spirit of God, they are the sons of God."* The Lord teaches us in His Word that sonship is manifested among the ones who are led by the Holy Spirit of God. It is the heart of the Father to father His sons and daughters in love. The Lord delights in leading us all throughout our lives lovingly and in every endeavor and dream that He's placed within our hearts to pursue. As we learn to live with our hearts beating as one with God, His desires become our desires because we are made one with Him. Therefore, we must be continually led by the Holy Spirit so that we ensure that no place is granted to our flesh to lead where our spirit is to go.

"We must lay it all down before we pick anything up." [2]

— NICHOLAS BARTA

Jesus modeled what perfect friendship is like with the Father, that in everything that He did, He was solely and completely led by Father God through the Holy Spirit in carrying out His Father's will. Jesus shows us that this friendship and fathering that he experienced with His heavenly Father is to be our model for abiding in a relationship with Him. Out of this beautiful place of being led by the Holy Spirit, we are simultaneously being fed with the bread of Heaven. It is in being fully led that we are truly fed the things of the Spirit, so that we walk in the Spirit and not in our flesh. For the things of the flesh lead to death, but the things of the Spirit lead to life (Rom 8:13).

This lifestyle of learning to be led in even the smallest of things will require a deeper level of humility for the greater things that God wants to release to us and through us. In this place, we discover how to surrender all our abilities, ambitions, motives, dreams, and capabilities to the Lord, allowing us to entrust everything we have to Him and be guided by His Holy Spirit in all our intentions. This is the pathway of sonship that will ensure that we are not misled by the things of the flesh nor deceived by the things of the enemy or the world. Living the abiding lifestyle is learning to be led and fed in all ways and all circumstances by the Lord so that we can live fueled by the Holy Spirit and led by Him into anything he calls us to do. The lifestyle led by the Holy Spirit is the most joyous, exciting, invigorating lifestyle full of surprises, excitement, and glory! When we truly learn to lay everything down, we are then enabled by the Holy Spirit to pick up what He's called us to carry. We must lay it all down before we pick anything up.

Honor Anchored In Humility

In everything we see through the life and leadership of Jesus, perhaps one of the most attractive qualities of Jesus, second to His perfect love for people, is the humility He showed. In order to increase our capacity for all that he's called us to carry and steward for His glory, we must exponentially increase in humility. Jesus is our perfect example of everything in life, and especially of what it looked like to grow in favor with God and favor with man moving with great power and authority that's anchored in love and humility. This same requirement by God is extended to us as His children who are called by Him to do the works that Jesus did, and even greater works because He goes to the Father (John 14:12). What an incredible invitation for ever-increasingly more than we could ever imagine is given to us through this truth in God's Word! In this declaration made by our Lord Jesus, there is also an unseen call to deepen our hearts into greater humility so that we may steward well the increase of His power and glory moving through us to heal, deliver, and set free the captives.

"Pray for the grace of humility." [3]

When I think of the prayers of hunger that people pray in wanting to see the greater things that Jesus spoke of and to see the dead raised, I can't help but say that first and most importantly, we must hunger to pray for the grace of humility. Without this grace, it can be easy for our flesh to mislead us and our minds to think that we had something to do with the miracles and signs that we witnessed the Lord working through our hands. With great power comes great responsibility to deepen humility. Deepening our friendship with the Lord is to always come before Him with pure hearts and clean hands (Ps 24:4).

"Humility is the key to accessing increase." [4]

— NICHOLAS BARTA

I believe it's most helpful to think of this like we would with our closest friends. The ones that are the absolute closest to you in your life will have the greatest access to information and invitations in your life. For instance, you would not give the keys to your house and your car and the most intimate details of your heart to someone you just met or to a friend who does not have that access to your life. These types of deep friendship privileges are cultivated over time where trust has been built, and the exchange of truth has been prioritized in all ways. Those are the friends that you would hand the keys to your house or car and have no second thought or worry about what they might do with it. A greater level of access is granted because of the trust that has been cultivated.

This is much like how it is with the Lord. With those who walk intimately with Him, He grants greater access to the things closest to His heart, and He entrusts greater anointing to move in greater power because of their humility of heart. Humility is the key to accessing increase. For one who has walked intimately with the Lord in close friendship, humility is the natural heart posture and dynamic of all interactions with the Lord. Greater blessings, greater anointing, and an increase in financial blessings have no change in a person's heart from understanding the level of love they are at because they are anchored in humility and a loving relationship with the Lord. When granted an increase from the Lord, the heart of one anchored in sonship will seek the heart of the Father in how He wants them to allocate those resources, funds, or blessings.

I once heard a quote that captures the heart of humility and has always stayed with me. My friend Chris Gore once said, "The more I see, the lower I get, and the lower I get, the more I see." Over all the years of ministry, this quote has stuck with me the most because just as Jesus grew in favor with God and in favor with man (Luke 2:52), we too can grow in that favor as we obey the Lord and intimately follow Him in close friendship so that His desires become our desires and His will becomes our prayer. In continually walking in this type of relationship anchored in humility, we'll surely yield the fruit of His blessings that He pours out on those who are faithful to do what He calls them to do. Then, our only response can be to give Him all the honor, all the glory, and all the praise because, since all is from Him, all must remain for Him.

> "As we remain in life union with Jesus, the supernatural becomes our natural."[5]

As we deepen our hearts of humility in our pursuit of giving God honor in all things, we will see more of the greater things that Jesus spoke of. As Chris hinted, as we see more of those things, we must exponentially increase in humility so that the new wine of blessings of miracles, signs, and wonders will not burst an old wineskin of yesterday's humility. As we remain in life union with Jesus, the supernatural becomes our natural. How is it possible that it could not be? If we become like the one we worship, and as we abide in the Lord, His supernatural life becomes fused together in life, which is in union with our lives. Then, the supernatural is made natural and will flow increasingly in conjunction with our hunger, humility, and honor in and for the Lord.

God's design for the infrastructure of stewarding this is in oneness relationship with Him that flows like the closest friendship beyond anything we could ever imagine with the God of all creation. Abba's father heart is that all His sons and daughters would discover this possibility of intimate, close friendship with Him so that we could operate from that place in all our affairs and endeavors in life. Life union with Jesus looks like a flourishing garden of friendship where we know what is closest and most dear to the heart of God. In this place, we will come to know His ways so that we can pray His will upon the earth in our every circumstance and situation.

9

ABIDING PRAYER

HEARTS BEATING AS ONE

There is an endless, eternal treasure of intimacy and revelation to be sought through a close friendship with the Lord as we come to know more of His heart. Knowing His heart causes us to be familiar with His ways. We will then be able to pray increasingly more of His will to be made manifest upon the Earth, praying what Jesus is praying for and in the way He is praying it.

Just imagine for a moment seeing an explosion of the growth of miracles, provision, breakthroughs, and answered prayer in your life. Imagine seeing the lame walk before your eyes, or seeing a friend in a desperate financial situation suddenly have a breakthrough as you prayed for them in faith. Likely you probably have multitudes of testimonies of God's goodness throughout your life, but what would an *explosion* of growth in the miraculous far beyond anything you've ever seen or dreamed of look like? I believe this is the Lord's invitation for us all to grow tremendously in the type of prayer life that Jesus shared with His Father: abiding prayer.

How beautiful is the heart of Father God to show us that there is no divide and no difference between the way He interacted with Jesus, His beloved Son, and the way He interacts with each one of us as His beloved sons and daughters?! As we look at the life and leadership of Jesus, we see what a perfect relationship looks like between a Father and His Son. Think of all the times that Jesus withdrew from the crowds to be with His Father in prayer. During these times of prayer, I imagine there was such a symphony of the oneness of Jesus' heart beating as one with His Father's heart, knowing His Father's will, and praying for it to be manifested.

As we have been deepening our understanding of the revelation given to us in John 15 about abiding, we see here that one of the greatest strengths of Jesus' ministry upon the Earth was found in His ability to abide in oneness with His Father. Jesus' sonship unto His Father was to spend time alone with Him, seek Him, and know His ways so that he would pray His Father's will, being confident that it would be granted. Through His time of intimate prayer, Jesus became intimately acquainted with His Father's heart, causing everything he did and said to flow in direct correlation with what he heard His Father speak and what he saw His Father reveal. Jesus reveals to us in John 15:7 that this same type of relational exchange is made completely available through the abiding.

> "If you abide in Me, and My words abide in you, you will ask what you desire, and it shall be done for you" (John 15:7).

As we read this verse, it may seem that what Jesus spoke is quite radical. However, we must not miss the first part of the verse, that as we *abide* in Jesus and that His words *abide* in us, we, out of that place, will then ask for the things that we desire, and Jesus assures us it will be done for us. The first part of this verse will cancel out anything of the flesh or the desires of the world because the condition is based upon abiding in Jesus with His Word alive and abiding in our hearts. God's Word will never contradict His will, and therefore, when His Word is alive in our hearts, the things that we desire will flow from His Word that are alive in us. Just as Jesus demonstrates a life where His heart beats as one with His Father, we too are invited into that place by His holy Blood to beat as one with the Father, the Son, and the Holy Spirit. With His Word alive in our hearts, our desires will be filtered through our life union with Jesus so that they are purified and flowing in alignment with His will for our lives. Therefore, Jesus says that out of the abiding, whatever we desire and ask for shall be done for us.

It's beautiful to see that in this verse, the lifestyle of sonship rooted in abiding will produce the fruit of purification of our desires and ambitions. In abiding in Jesus, the true vine, His Spirit is alive in us and filters through the things of the flesh as we follow the Holy Spirit's leading in life. We are not expected nor required to try in our own strength to pursue the will of the Father and pray perfectly according to His will. We are not expected to filter through the desires of the flesh or what seem to be our own good thoughts that may be contrary to God's will. The greatest gift of the Holy Spirit is alive inside of us to help us pursue the Lord, seek His will, and pray His ways. Jesus says this about the Holy Spirit in John 16:13-15,

> "However, when He, the Spirit of truth, has come, He will guide you into all truth; for He will not speak on His own *authority*, but whatever He hears He will speak; and He will tell you things to come. He will glorify Me, for He will take of what is Mine and declare it to you. All things that the Father has are Mine. Therefore I said that He will take of Mine and declare *it* to you" (John 16:13-15).

All that Jesus has is made available and given fully to us as inheritance through the Holy Spirit. The lifestyle of sonship abiding in Jesus is entrusting the Holy Spirit to lead and guide us in the way we are to go with His counseling eye upon us (Ps 32:8). In this place, God's desires are being manifested to us and becoming our desires as we remain in life union with Jesus. Jesus is the pathway of life unto the Father and is the only way to Him. As we continue deepening our relationship with the Lord Jesus, the Son of God, we will come to know the life of living as a son or daughter unto our Heavenly Father. That lifestyle of sonship through abiding prayer will dramatically increase the incredible things you will see God do through your surrendered life.

Teach Us To Pray

Let's take a moment to travel back in time to the days when Jesus walked on the earth with His disciples. Picture the sights, sounds, and smells of early living in the days of Jesus and His disciples. Have you ever thought about what it was like for the disciples to walk with Jesus and minister with Him for those three years? I can only imagine how incredible that must have been! Being able first-hand to see Jesus heal the multitudes of innumerable kinds of sicknesses and diseases, to see the demon-possessed set free, the lame walk, the blind see, and even the dead to be raised.

Fathom for a moment what encountering the glory of the Lord in that place must have been like. I'm sure there would be many questions running through your mind as you witness the Lord do the 'impossible' right before your eyes. Yet, the disciples who walked with Jesus day by day could distinguish a direct correlation between Jesus' ability to work miracles and His prayer life with His Father. The disciples recognized the pattern of Jesus withdrawing from the crowds and even from them to be with His Father in prayer. They noticed as Jesus prayed late into the night or was up in the wee hours of the morning that the authority and power to work miracles directly flowed from Jesus' prayer life. We see the one thing in the Gospels that the disciples asked Jesus how to do. It wasn't how to work the miracles, how to raise the dead, or how to open blind eyes or deaf ears. The one thing they had asked Jesus how to do was how to pray. Matthew 6 captures Jesus teaching His disciples some incredible principles about prayer. He starts off by setting the standard that our good deeds and prayer life should always flow from the secret place with our heavenly Father. Jesus says in Matthew 6:6,

> "But you, when you pray, go into your room, and when you have shut your door, pray to your Father who *is* in the secret *place*; and your Father who sees in secret will reward you openly" (Matt 6:6).

Jesus teaches that our prayer life is to flow in and from the secret place of intimacy exchanged one-on-one with the Lord of all creation. Flowing from this intimacy is the flowing fountain of a flourishing prayer life. It is inviting Him into the garden of your heart in all things and all ways through everything in life, allowing Him to guide and father us in all our affairs in life. It is this relational exchange of communication through abiding prayer that creates a flourishing release of rewards of God's blessing into our lives.

In all the times we read through Scripture how Jesus withdrew from the crowds and from His disciples to be with His Father, we see that there was greater authority, anointing, and intimacy that flowed from that secret place of prayer with His heavenly Father. God's secrets are released in the secret place, and that is the place where friendship is built and cultivated through intimate communication in oneness with God. Prayer is a heart-flowing communication of pressing in face-to-face and heart-to-heart with the Lord where we share the things on our hearts while asking Him for guidance and wisdom as well as pursue listening to the things on His heart about what He is speaking to us about. Listening to the voice of the Father attunes us to learn more about His heart so that we can pray for His will to be done upon the earth.

Jesus continues to instruct His disciples, including every follower of Christ after that, on how we are to pray.

> "In this manner, therefore, pray:
> Our Father in heaven,
> Hallowed be Your name.
> Your kingdom come.
> Your will be done
> On earth as *it is* in heaven.
> Give us this day our daily bread.
> And forgive us our debts,
> As we forgive our debtors.
> And do not lead us into temptation,
> But deliver us from the evil one.
> For Yours is the kingdom and the power and the glory forever. Amen."
> (Matt 6:9-13)

When we look deeper at the Lord's prayer, we can see the evidence of intimacy woven all throughout. Jesus begins this section by saying, therefore, in this manner, pray. We read in Matthew 6:1-8 that Jesus is referring to praying in such a manner that is free from vain repetition and prideful ambition. These are two key things that give us the scope of direction for abiding prayer that our hearts must be free from in order to pray in the way Jesus prayed.

In verse 9, we read how Jesus acknowledges His Father and how we too, are to acknowledge the Father and the absolute purity and holiness of His name. This word hallowed shows a complete sanctifying, a setting apart from Yahweh from anything and everything that is unclean. Jesus is showing us we are to lift high and exalt the name of God, being completely set apart from anything and everything in this life and world. We are to lift high the name of King Jesus and the Lordship of our God, high above everything in our minds and our hearts as we pursue praying.

In verse ten, Jesus teaches us to declare and call forth the Kingdom of God has come and the will of God to be done upon the Earth in the same way and fashion as it is done in heaven. This is a powerful declaration of the will of God to be made manifest in our lives and our circumstances. Jesus is teaching His disciples, including us today, that it is the holy will of God that will bring forth the transformation upon the Earth from the heavenly realm of His glory. Acknowledging the will of God that is pure, holy, and completely set apart sets us in a place of sonship with submission and sacrifice. As we pray for the will of God to be made manifest in our lives, there is a holy exchange of our complete submission to His will and sacrifice of the surrender of everything else contrary to His will. This can include our own thoughts and ambitions on what we think we need to pray or how we think the situation needs to be dealt with in a specific scope of outcome in our minds of answered prayer. This involves saying from our hearts, "Father, I cannot discern in my flesh and ability Your will, so I surrender to You and say, let Your will be done and let Your kingdom come in and through my life for Your glory!" In surrendering in this way, we are letting go of the way we think things should be or the outcome we believe should come, and we are surrendering completely to the Lordship of God. In exchange, God promises us many things in His Word, one of which is shalom peace, which will surpass all of our understanding and create a safeguard for our minds and our hearts. As we pray the Lord's prayer in faith, we are praying in a manner of believing and declaring that the earth will look like and operate like heaven.

> "Be anxious for nothing, but in everything by prayer and supplication, with thanksgiving, let your requests be made known to God;

and the peace of God, which surpasses all understanding, will
guard your hearts and minds through Christ Jesus" (Phil 4:6-7).

In verse 11, we must live by fresh daily bread and not by yesterday's revelation. Living in oneness daily with fresh revelation is to receive Jesus afresh as our daily bread. Just as the Israelites were commanded by the Lord in the wilderness not to collect and store manna on the Sabbath, we are to live with the fresh bread of Jesus in our hearts every day. In John 4:34, Jesus reveals that to do His Father's will is His daily bread. In crying out to the Father to give us our daily bread, we are asking the Lord for His fresh bread of making His Son manifest in our lives so that we can abide in Him and learn the will and way of almighty God through the indwelling of the Holy Spirit.

Following this in verse 12, we are to pray for forgiveness of all our wrongdoings and sins so that our hearts are made clean and pure. This is a crucial part of prayer. As we come to the Lord in His presence seeking to pray His will upon the Earth, we must do so with clean hands and a pure heart (Ps 24:4). For instance, nobody would take some coffee beans and grind them up fresh ready to brew some coffee and place those grinds on moldy old grinds in a dirty filter. To do so would be to *compromise the purity* of those clean, fresh coffee grinds and taint them with the moldy old coffee grinds in the dirty filter, thus contaminating the whole batch. So it is the same in prayer, that we are to have the pure revelation released to us by the Holy Spirit to flow through a clean filter of our hearts so that we pray the will of the Father with clean hands and a pure heart. Forgiveness is God's instrument for cleansing our hearts from sin and impurities, and it also graces us with the ability to forgive others so that the filter of our hearts is not contaminated with the pollution of unforgiveness.

The Lord Jesus finishes teaching us in verse 13 to pray that we would not be led into temptation, evil, offenses, and impurities of the enemy's influence in life and this world. We are to ask the Lord to guard us and protect us from being led by the deceitfulness of riches, worldliness, or our own fleshly desires that oppose the pure will of God. The prayer continues that we would be delivered from such evils originating from our enemy, the devil. This deliverance prayer is also intended to deliver us from any worries, doubts, anxieties, depression, disappointments, bondage, and any other thing that would deter us from the ways and will of God. This is the heart's cry through prayer that we would be set free! From this new freedom, we declare the Lord's complete dominion, authority, and rulership over everything.

We attribute everything pertaining to godliness and holiness to the glory of the Lord as we proclaim His Lordship in all the land and every situation ending with amen, so be it! As we pray the Lord's prayer with pure hearts and clean hands, we are not using vain repetition as the Lord Jesus had warned us in the previous verses, but we are aligning our hearts with the Kingdom of Heaven and with the absolute Lordship of Jesus over our lives and everything. This alignment of our hearts is essential for us to be cleansed, attuned, and in the right position to pray for God's Kingdom to rule and reign in our situations and circumstances.

Alignment of Desires & Ambitions

One aspect of the benefits of walking in sonship that I find so amazing is God's supernatural ability to work deep within our hearts to bring alignment with His will. It seems just amazing that in a moment's time, my heart posture concerning something could be strongly bent one way, then in the next moment, after yielding everything afresh over to Jesus, He completely changes my perspective and motives while bringing deep alignment within my heart unto His will. We know that in and of ourselves, we do not know how to pray as we ought (Rom 8:26-27). There is no one walking the earth who would not need to be aware of the deceits of the ambitions and the misleading of the flesh. Every single human being has a potential and a propensity to bend toward that which his or her heart desires from the flesh. Acknowledging this potential is not to invoke shame or to live with a handicap to it but to instill a deeper longing to embrace humility and lay everything down at the feet of Jesus, allowing Him to align and redirect our hearts. With our hearts realigned, we can walk with a holy ambition to pursue God's will. When we hunger for and embrace that spirit of humility, we position ourselves to receive God's Kingdom alive in our hearts and flowing through our prayers.

Let me share a story of a time when the Holy Spirit taught me a deeper level of walking in abiding prayer. I had received a message from a loved one that a person within our extended community was now in hospice care. Although my heart felt saddened by the news, my spirit felt excited about what the Lord was about to do! Upon arriving at the hospital's hospice care center, I was greeted by loved ones and brought back to our beloved sister's room, where I found her hooked up to several medical devices, including a breathing machine. The situation on the surface looked impossible, but I knew in my heart that God could do anything.

I began drawing on numerous testimonies in my mind of God working healing miracles I had witnessed firsthand in the past and my faith began to rise to pray for this daughter to be healed and raised up. I was confident that God could work a miracle here and bring Himself such glory. However, I felt the Holy Spirit nudge my heart and say, "Ask Me how you are to pray." So, I prayed and asked Him, and what He revealed surprised me. He instructed me to pray that she would be prepared to be received by the King. The Lord wasn't desiring us to pray for her healing, but to pray for her transition into heaven.

What took place shortly after the Lord gave this direction was nothing short of glorious! As we were praying, God released prophetic insight over this woman's life of things I had never known. What had happened following praying the way Jesus led me to pray was the shalom peace of God. The Prince of Peace Himself filled that room with His glorious presence. There was the holy awe of God that was so tangible and potent in that room where the joy of the Lord and His peace that surpasses all understanding filled that place as the atmosphere completely shifted.

I remember seeing visions of this daughter dancing gloriously as a little girl before her heavenly Father. The Holy Spirit stirred in my heart to prophesy over her that the Lord Jesus was handing her dancing shoes and inviting her to dance again with Him. God's holy presence increased as we all were in awe of Him and all that He was speaking prophetically about this daughter of His.

The joy was unspeakable in that atmosphere, and we all carried that joy in our hearts, knowing this beloved daughter was being fully prepared to get ready to meet Jesus face to face. Although there had been no more responsiveness from her for the whole day, her spirit was responding to what was being released in that room, and even though she was virtually unconscious, her face began smiling gloriously! I also later found out that when she was little, she had loved to dance but had given it up at a young age, probably because of a lack of support from her parents. Jesus was dancing with her in that room and romancing her as she began letting go of this life and preparing to meet Him in heaven face to face.

We all began rejoicing, singing, and prophesying over our beloved sister as God worked this miracle before our eyes. I can only imagine what she began to see and witness during that incredible time of dancing with Jesus! The Lord was restoring her innocence and childlikeness back to her in that time in His glory. It was as if she was being completely healed spiritually while being prepared to be joined with the King for all eternity. It was just a few short days later that our beloved sister transitioned from this life and was brought into her eternal destination in heaven with the Lord. I thank God for this encounter and give Him glory for all He did in this beautiful time of prayer with our beloved sister.

"Assumption can be an enemy to abiding prayer because it's rooted in the flesh and is reliant upon our ability apart from God." [1]

— NICHOLAS BARTA

Through this testimony, the Lord taught me some important lessons about the alignment of our hearts with His will in prayer. He taught me about the complete surrendering of self-reliance through flesh guidance in prayer. I never want my prayers to be in contrast to what the Lord is praying for or how He is asking me to pray. Assumption can be an enemy to abiding prayer because it's rooted in the flesh and is reliant upon our ability apart from God. When we're in abiding prayer, you can see that if I had just prayed out of my flesh, I would have just prayed for a healing miracle and gone after that because I've experienced healing and seen God work miracles so many times before. If I had prayed that prayer, I would have been moved in the flesh and not been aligned in the spirit. However, when we're living in a life union with Jesus, the fragrance of His love, the potency of His presence, and the life source of Jesus Himself are getting into the roots in our hearts, providing the nutrients of Him into our lives in the soil of intimacy. Therefore, in praying this way, we'll begin producing fruit, and out of that fruit comes this abiding prayer into producing fruit that will remain.

What was so beautiful about this story was that through abiding prayer, as we prayed in the spirit and worshiped in the spirit, the Holy Spirit generated the alignment of our spirit, soul (our mind, will, and emotions), and body to be in full alignment with that life union with Jesus. In this alignment, we were then flowing from a place of prayer that was in unison with what Jesus was praying and what the Holy Spirit was uttering inside of us. As a result, there was a river of intercession coming out of abiding oneness where Father God says 'yes' and 'amen' to all His promises as we align ourselves with His Spirit, joining in with the intercession of Jesus that's always aligned in sonship to the Father (2 Cor 1:20). Alignment with the heart and will of God releases a river of prayer and intercession that breaks open the heavens and brings God's answers to our prayers. Our major role is to depend completely upon and yield totally over to the Lordship of the Holy Spirit in us to bring about His work through us.

> "Likewise the Spirit also helps in our weaknesses. For we do not know what we should pray for as we ought, but the Spirit Himself makes intercession for us with groanings which cannot be uttered" (Rom 8:26).

In this verse, when we realize that in our own human tendencies and through our own flesh, many times, our flesh gets in the way. This is where we're not actually lined up in that abiding prayer, because when we're operating in the flesh, we're praying either our own desires or the way we think something should be. If we pray under assumption based upon our experience, we pray through tradition and not through fresh revelation brought by the Holy Spirit found in abiding.

We see in Romans 8:26 that the Holy Spirit also helps in our weaknesses, and every single one of us has weaknesses that can become areas for growth in prayer. For we do not know what we should pray for as we ought, but it is the Holy Spirit Himself who makes intercession for us with groanings that cannot be uttered. It is the Holy Spirit inside of us that is percolating those prayer points of the will of the Father, and abiding in Jesus will bring them to manifest in our lives through the Holy Spirit!

Whenever we're praying, flowing from the Holy Spirit, we pray that life source of an abundance of Jesus into the situation or circumstance. It is the leadership of the Holy Spirit inside of us in response to our surrendering to Him who makes known what we are to pray as we ought, as our spirits are brought in alignment with Jesus. Abiding prayer is where we pray in the spirit without ceasing, which is literally anchoring in oneness with Jesus, Abba, and the Holy Spirit dwelling inside you. This is the fullness of God Himself through the Holy Spirit in such powerful prayer that it breaks open the heavens, and God's answers to prayer are released.

When you're anchored in living in life union with Jesus, you know that His Holy Spirit inside of you makes intercession with deep groaning, including immeasurable passion and fervency. When we're living and abiding in the true vine, Jesus makes known to us what He's praying for, and the Holy Spirit bears witness to our spirit with Jesus' intercession and brings us into alignment and agreement with that abiding prayer. From this place, we're now praying what Jesus is praying, and we're praying and declaring through what the Holy Spirit inside of us is praying, which is in total alignment with the Father's will.

I've seen times in my life where I prayed in the flesh and certainly did not see the result or the outcome manifest in the way I had planned in my mind. Yet I've also seen many times in my life where the Holy Spirit was teaching me to pray as I ought. These times in abiding prayer were the most fruitful in my life, where what I was led to pray and how I was led to pray lined up with God's will and therefore led to pray His will in the situation. The Holy Spirit taught me to search and ask what and how Jesus was praying for the situation. It was so much simpler, and I was not self-reliant on my ability to discern and sift through what I thought was His way of praying in complex situations. The Lord said to ask Him simply, "Lord, what are You praying about this situation, and how can I partner with You?" This relieved all the pressure of trying to figure everything out in my strength apart from sonship, and it placed me in a position to rely fully on Him in sonship that's anchored in His strength and ability.

I don't know if this has been the case in your life, but I have certainly seen such an acceleration in answered prayer in this place of abiding prayer. As we're abiding in Jesus, we are asking Him what and how to pray for situations so that we're partnering with His prayers through our sanctified mouths. Suddenly, in this place, the prayers don't need to be so long. The prayers are powerful and are flowing in oneness from the heart of the Father through the Holy Spirit in us. This is where we see Jesus do what He can do by bringing answers to those prayers in incredible ways that we didn't expect, because it's in alignment with the heart and will of our amazing Heavenly Father.

Encounter Time

Son or daughter, choose to cry out in deep hunger for the Father to form you into a man or woman of abiding prayer. Ask Him to mold, shape, prune, and tend to you to form you into a person of abiding prayer who listens to His heart, knows His ways, and prays His will. I believe that as a result, you will see a great increase of answered prayer in and through your life as you remain closely and intimately joined to Jesus in oneness.

Take a moment right now to invite the Holy Spirit. Draw on the confidence of knowing that you are indeed His beloved child whom He loves and is well pleased with. Rest in that place of relational intimacy and security with and in the Lord. Now ask Him, "Holy Spirit, what's one thing that you are praying for me that I can come into alignment and agreement with?" Grab a pen and journal and write whatever He speaks to you. What He reveals may directly contrast with what you've believed about yourself and your situation(s). This is a holy confrontation that will displace the leaven of the enemy and of the world where we've believed and prayed contrary to God's will or neglected to pray to bring ourselves in alignment with what the Lord wants us to pray. Do not resist Him, but embrace all He shows you and pray as He directs you. Write declarations you can declare over yourself in alignment with this newfound truth. Declare God's truth and pray it daily over yourself, and note how the Holy Spirit transforms you and your heart and mind. Give Him thanks and praise for speaking His truth over you!

Now, take another moment to posture your heart and ask the Holy Spirit what He is praying over a loved one you've been praying for. Ask Jesus, "Lord, what is Your heart for this person? How do You see them, and how can I pray for them in alignment with your prayers?" Write all that the Lord reveals to you and align your prayers with Him in great faith, knowing that with God, ALL things are possible (Matt 19:26)! Write some declarations from Scripture that He highlights to you that you can pray and declare over this person or people.

Practice this lifestyle of sonship and abiding prayer every day and every time as situations and prayer needs arise in your family, workplace, city, or nation. Allow the Holy Spirit to mold you into a mighty man or woman of prayer who seeks His will and ways in all things. You will flow closer and closer to the heart of the Father, and He indeed will share His secrets with you in the secret place as you purely pursue His heart and His ways in and through abiding prayer. As you practice this more and more in your daily life in your walk with Jesus, fruitfulness will increase and abound because it's being cultivated out of abiding in the Lord. May you see even more breakthroughs and great triumphs through your surrendered prayer life of abiding in the true vine!

Daily Prayer For Alignment In Abiding Prayer

Holy Spirit, I welcome You right now. I thank you so much that you are praying for each of us since before time was. Thank You for never stopping to pray for us! I thank You, Holy Spirit, that You live inside me as a born-again believer in Jesus Christ my Lord. Holy Spirit, I pray right now that You would bring revelation to me and that You would reveal to me Your heart so that I may seek You, Lord, and become aligned with Your prayers. Help me, Lord, to pray Your will according to the way You pray it, in alignment with Jesus's prayers in the Father's will. I pray that, as a result, I will bear more fruit and fruit that remains. Holy Spirit, I pray You would show me what Jesus is praying so I can align with what You are praying and pray that into being. I declare Your Kingdom come, and Your will be done on Earth as it is in heaven! I give You all the honor and praise, and I thank You, Jesus, so much that You're always with me, that You never leave me nor forsake me, for I am living in life union in and with You as my true vine and life source. I declare that unto You belongs all the glory, praise, and honor in the beautiful name of Jesus, I pray. Amen.

"Rejoice always, pray without ceasing, give thanks in all circumstances; for this is the will of God in Christ Jesus for you. Do not quench the Spirit" (1 Thess 5:16-19 ESV).

10

TRIALS INTO TRIUMPHS
CHOSEN AND SET APART

There is one thing that you can count on that is certain and true for your life, and that is that you were born for such a time as this! That you are alive, and breathing is pure evidence that God has a plan for your life and a destiny for you to fulfill. Jesus teaches us that in this life, we will experience trials and tribulation, but that we are to remain anchored in the truth that His victory reigns eternal forever and ever over every situation, life circumstance, national crisis, and global event (John 16:33). We remember that in Him we are chosen, and we are set apart from the world and everything in it.

God is beckoning out to the Body of Christ, that in these last days, we are to remain abiding in the true vine of His Son, Jesus. Our Lord Jesus called and marked us as sons and daughters to live in His triumph, even amid battles, trials, and tribulations. Jesus prepared His disciples just as He is preparing us today, as He spoke in John 15:18-19 that we will be hated by the world and reviled just as Jesus was.

> "If the world hates you, you know that it hated Me before *it hated* you. If you were of the world, the world would love its own. Yet because you are not of the world, but I chose you out of the world, therefore the world hates you" (John 15:18-19).

We are chosen by Him to be found in Him so that our witness to the world resounds the triumph of the Lamb over every false authority, demonic stronghold, and every ruler of darkness. Jesus teaches us we will be hated and rejected by the world because we are the sons and daughters of light who are swimming upstream against the current of the deception, sin, and deceitfulness of this world. Do not think for a moment that you are called to 'fit in' to this worldly system of Babylon. No, beloved sons and daughters, we are called to stand out and shine for the King of Glory! Jesus has chosen us out of the world so we can be set apart for His purposes and glory through our surrendered lives upon the earth. Therefore, as sons and daughters of the King, we are not 'ground-bound' in the trials and hardships that we face in this life. Rather, we are caught up in oneness unto the LORD, where we live and reign with God in our heavenly position seated in Christ.

Seated IN Christ

> "But God, who is rich in mercy, because of His great love with which He loved us, even when we were dead in trespasses, made us alive together with Christ (by grace you have been saved), and raised *us* up together, and made *us* sit together in the heavenly *places* in Christ Jesus" (Eph 2:4-6).

Throughout several years, I have preached and taught this passage from time to time. I would quote that we are seated *with* Christ in the heavenly places. It wasn't until years later that the Holy Spirit highlighted to me I had been quoting this passage incorrectly. He lovingly showed me that the text in the New King James Version clearly says that we are seated *together* in the heavenly places *in* Christ Jesus. This changed everything for me because he allowed me to see His heart expressed in oneness through this passage. The heart of the Father is that we are caught up together in oneness in him and from that place of our heavenly position seated in Christ, we are to rule and reign by His power and in His authority and for His glory in this life. 1 John 4:17 says, "Love has been perfected among us in this: that we may have boldness in the day of judgment; because as He is, so are we in this world."

God is teaching His sons and daughters in His Word that just as His Son Jesus was in this life and how He completely lived abiding in oneness with His Father, we are to abide in Him, live through Him, and unto Him in all things. From this standpoint of realized position, we understand that we have access to every spiritual blessing in the heavenly places.

Every Spiritual Blessing

As we grasp the revelation that our true position in the spirit is that we are seated in Christ, we understand more so that all that Christ has is made fully available to us by living through Him. Paul wrote earlier in Ephesians 1:3,

> "Blessed *be* the God and Father of our Lord Jesus Christ, who has blessed us with every spiritual blessing in the heavenly *places* in Christ" (Eph 1:3).

Notice again how the Lord shows us in His Word that we have access to every spiritual blessing in the heavenly places IN Christ. We are not to be living separated from the true vine in our trials and hardships in this life, but we are to live from our heavenly position in Christ Jesus, accessing all that He is into all that we are so that we can pray His Kingdom to come and His will be done upon the Earth in whatever situations we face. The Holy Spirit is the power of God being made manifest through us with our alignment with the will of the Father and the Word of His Son. The Holy Spirit takes our prayers mixed with His in us and through us and bursts forth into action with great power to carry out the will of God into the world.

This is the place where we will see great triumphs come because of our trials. His Kingdom is established as every false authority and demonic throne is brought down by the power of God through our agreement with Him. We must live with the revelation that we are indeed blessed, and in that blessing is the *release* of every spiritual blessing of anything and everything we could need to rise in victory in this life through the Blood of the Lamb. We are to take the standard of the cross of Jesus Christ and the victory of absolute triumph He won for all eternity, and to place that cross in our foresight in front of any situation or circumstance that we face. Think of it this way: take any thought, mindset, or belief you have, line it up with the 'cross hairs' of the cross of Jesus, and 'pull the trigger.' Anything that is not in alignment with God's truth through the finished work of Jesus Christ on the cross will be exposed and eliminated! Abba Father wants us to call upon Him and work together in partnership with Him to pray, decree, and call those things that aren't as though they were so that everything comes into alignment with the cross (see Rom 4:17).

During a season when the Lord was deepening my and my wife's understanding of our authority in Christ, we got to see the manifested reality of our prayers with a visible breakthrough in the land. On one of our regular routes, while driving to an appointment, the Holy Spirit had highlighted this strange house surrounded by dead trees that hid in plain sight. God had revealed to my wife that this was a demonic stronghold that was owned by a person, most likely a witch or warlock, who was heavily operating in the occult. We'd seen a car normally parked there, so we knew it was owned by someone.

After the Holy Spirit showed us this false authority stronghold, we prayed in the spirit that it would be demolished, along with all the curses and demonic influence broken off the land. Within a few short months later, as we were driving to our appointment, to our surprise, out of nowhere, the building was being bulldozed to the ground along with every dead tree torn down! There was nothing left of this demonic stronghold as God had responded to our prayers and tore down that which had plagued His land. We rejoiced and gave God glory as we watched the territory being demolished over that next week. We did not stop there at the demolition but pressed in prayer and continually prophesied with our kids that this land would be redeemed and used for the Kingdom of God to further the Gospel of Jesus Christ! As of writing this, we are waiting expectantly for the manifestation of what the Lord is going to establish on that land for His glory!

What we learned through this is that while we are abiding in close intimacy with Jesus being seated in Him in the heavenly places, He will show us assignments where He wants us to take the authority that He's given us and pray His will into existence allowing His Kingdom to come and be established in the land. God is simply looking for the ones who will declare, as Isaiah declared, "Here I am, Lord, send me" (Isaiah 6:8)! As we go in obedience, Christ's triumph is released through us to bring Kingdom breakthrough and change.

The Aroma Of Christ

We are assured because of Jesus' eternal victory at Calvary, that God is the One who will lead us in triumph in Christ. 2 Corinthians 2:14 says,

> "Now thanks *be* to God who always leads us in triumph in Christ, and through us diffuses the fragrance of His knowledge in every place" (2 Cor 2:14).

No matter how difficult or impossible the situation may seem, in Christ and with Christ, we are assured that God will lead us in triumph. Our role in this place is to have faith, to agree with God's will, and to pray His way to be made manifest into that which we believe for Him to move upon, just like the story of the bulldozing. As we come into agreement with our faith mixed as we pray, God diffuses the aroma of knowledge in every place. In the next two verses, we will learn exactly what that aroma is.

> "For we are to God the fragrance of Christ among those who are being saved and among those who are perishing. To the one *we are* the aroma of death *leading* to death, and to the other the aroma of life *leading* to life" (2 Cor 2:15-16).

The deeper meaning and revelation through the historical context here is quite compelling. Here, Paul is writing about and referring to a Roman triumph procession where they would host a large victory parade when conquering one of their enemies. In this victory parade, both the conquering army and the captives from the opposing army were present where spices were burnt in celebration of the conquest. These burning spices released an aroma that was pleasing in celebration to the people of the conquering party, but to those who were captive and had been conquered, it was a terrible aroma, leading to a mindset of defeat, bondage and death.

Paul uses this depiction to illustrate the victorious sons and daughters of God walking in the triumph of Jesus Christ and the aroma of victory being dispersed throughout the Earth. To the ones who are being saved, it is a glorious, most wonderful aroma of life and a mental depiction of glorious eternal life to come. To those who are lost or who oppose the Gospel of Jesus Christ, it is an aroma of spiritual death leading to judgment and ultimate eternal separation from God.

I remember a time when I was at a local ministry and was caught up in a time of intercession with some other young adults. We prayed earnestly for our city and state, and God's presence seemed to increase exponentially. As we pressed in further, praying God's will for our state, all three of us were delightfully interrupted by the incredible aroma that filled the room. Now, it was just the three of us, and we had been there praying for about an hour with no one coming in or going out of that room. Finally, one of us broke the silence and said, "Oh my goodness, do you guys smell that?" All three of us confirmed we smelled this incredible floral, fruity smell. We stopped praying and began delighting in this incredible aroma. The presence of the Holy Spirit filled the room, and we knew Jesus had walked into that place with us. Although the smell was short-lived, it was so potent and intoxicating with the presence of Jesus. We were all overwhelmed by what the Lord had just done and in awe of our God!

There was a second time that the Lord manifested His aroma in the same ministry years later, where the room was filled with sons and daughters who loved the Lord as we were gathering for a training event. The small basement was filled with about 30 people of various ages, from young adults to the elderly. When our leader was speaking and ministering, this wonderful aroma swept through the room. I began looking around the room and saw some of the other young adults looking around in the same way I was. It was the most incredible floral, sweet smell that filled your whole being.

I looked around, seeing if it was a scented candle or perhaps someone's perfume, but found nothing that would equate to the strength and potency of this mysterious, wonderful aroma that came out of nowhere. I asked, this time keeping my voice quiet to one of the other young adults, "Do you smell that?" To my delight, the reply was a resounding, "Yes!" At the end of that gathering, several of us young adults had gathered together and talked about that sweet aroma, concluding that all of us had smelt it at the same time. We knew that Jesus Himself manifested Himself and released an aroma that night. Once again, we were in awe of God's holy presence.

I will never forget that sweet aroma. I long to encounter the Lord again in a way like that. Although I do not know why the Lord manifested Himself uniquely that night in that way, what I do know is that it was 100 percent supernatural. We encountered the aroma of the Lord Jesus, which led to life and pursuing a hunger for more of Jesus alive in our hearts.

Our lives, through abiding in Jesus Christ, will contain and release the aroma of Him into everything we touch in this life. As we abide in Him and His words abide in us, through our prayers, the aroma of the victory and triumph of Christ is released and made known in the heavenlies and upon the earth. We are indeed seated in Christ in the heavenly places, so we are seated in eternal victory and are to live *from* His victory, not *for* His victory in our lives. We understand that in Christ, all things are completed, and therefore, our portion is to believe and have faith, come into full agreement, and pray with our God-given authority from our heavenly position in Christ Jesus, accessing every spiritual blessing that is needed to accomplish victory in every situation. From this kingly royal position of great authority, we are to pray, decree, and pronounce God's Kingdom upon the earth through the authority of His Holy Spirit living in us. Therefore, our confidence anchored in sonship is not to be upon ourselves or our own ability to pray or generate victory in either, but to rest in our position in Christ, seeking Him for direction and guidance in the journey so that we can partner and co-labor with Christ to bring about His victory for His glory!

Co-laboring With Christ

One of my favorite aspects of understanding our sonship unto the Lord in accordance with prayer is that we labor together in unity and oneness in and with Jesus to bring His Kingdom upon the earth. We know from Romans 8:15 that we have been given the Spirit of adoption and have been completely fused together with the Lord by the Holy Spirit living in us. This passage picks up in verses 16 and 17, revealing that we are God's very own children and are, therefore, beneficiaries and inheritors together with Christ.

> "The Spirit Himself bears witness with our spirit that we are children of God, and if children, then heirs—heirs of God and joint heirs with Christ, if indeed we suffer with *Him*, that we may also be glorified together" (Rom 8:16-17).

It is in and through the Holy Spirit that our inheritance as heirs of God is made manifest together with and in Christ Jesus. We now can understand that the fullness of all that Jesus is and all that He has is made fully available to each of us through abiding in Him. We are not operating apart from God but abiding in God and through God to bring the revelation and manifestation of Jesus Christ, the Savior of the world, into the four corners of the world. In being joint heirs with Jesus, God is teaching us in His Word that all that was given to Jesus, His Son, is also given to us in Him. In ourselves, we can do absolutely nothing. But as we abide in Jesus, the fullness of His lordship, leadership, anointing and authority can flow through us as we take our authority through our position seated in Him and pray the Father's will to be done upon the Earth.

There will be trials and hardships, losses, disappointments, and suffering that will require a deeper maturity from us as we understand that just as Jesus was in this world, we are too. But in verse 17, we also see that as we're anchored in oneness with Jesus, we will be glorified together in Him and with Him. All things are from Him, so all things must remain unto Him. In Christ and through Christ and with Christ is the fullness of God's Kingdom, and the heart of the Father has expressed through His Word that we are indeed His children, and if His children, we are indeed heirs of His Kingdom. 1 Corinthians 3:9 says it clearly,

> "For we are God's fellow workers; you are God's field, *you are* God's building" (1Cor 3:9).

Together, as the Body of Christ unified by the Holy Spirit, we are being knitted and fitted together as God's house upon the earth. Each of us is a field with soft, fertile soil for the planting of the Lord. Whenever we pray, we are praying in unity with the Lord as heirs of His Kingdom to see His Kingdom come and His will be done for the glory of King Jesus! We may not see the result that we believe in, but we must remain confident of the spiritual truth that it is impossible to pray and have nothing happen. In this life, we will have trials, hardships, distresses, losses, disappointments, and suffering. We are assured, though, that even though we share in the sufferings of Christ, we also will share in His glory. Romans 8:18 says,

> "For I consider that the sufferings of this present time are not worthy *to be compared* with the glory which shall be revealed in us" (Rom 8:18).

Even though we will experience suffering in this life, the comparison to the manifest glory of God revealed in us and through us is far exceeding beyond anything we can imagine. God's glory revealed in us is the manifested greatness of Christ in you being expressed through you, which is the hope of glory (Col 1:27)! His glory being manifested and revealed through us can only come through our abiding in Him. It is in living life in Him that His life will be lived through us. As we remain abiding in Him even in times of great trial and hardship, Christ is being formed in us for the glory of God. Even in the hardest of situations where things seem completely hopeless, these are the moments where the glory of Christ can be magnified and shine the brightest.

One story I will never forget is from papa Leif Hetland, when he shared a story about a trip to the Middle East where he and his team had spent a year organizing a huge healing crusade where the gospel of Jesus Christ would be shared in a Muslim city of a completely unreached people group. Tens of thousands of dollars were spent to rent the field and all the equipment to organize and host this crusade. Leif shared that leading up to this crusade, before he departed from the United States, the spiritual warfare was intense, unlike any other trip. In battling through sickness, transportation issues, weather-related closures, and national upheaval, Leif continued pressing through the spiritual resistance, working toward the assignment the Lord had given of reaching this unreached people group with the Gospel.

In battling all these things, along with increased treacherous weather, he finally arrived within reaching distance of the field where they were to host this crusade. After all these things and being so close, his director informed him they had to cancel the event because of massive flooding in the field. At this darkest moment, when all hope seemed lost and all the funds and time expensed for the event were lost in a moment, Leif sought the Lord for His council and direction. To say that there was disappointment is a tremendous understatement, given the hardship and losses in this journey. But as Leif heroically placed his trust in the Lord and sought His counsel, beauty sprang forth from the ashes.

When all had seemed lost and the funds and time invested to reach these people were canceled at the last moment, God was working on something far greater that could not be seen. When this door had closed, God had opened an unseen door of unimaginable favor. Leif shared about attending a religious leader's wedding on this trip and other connections that were opened up that otherwise would have been closed. These connections that were made during this time had opened up supernatural doors of opportunity in the years that followed that granted tremendous, unprecedented favor with top government officials and religious leaders that are paving the way for the gospel to reach far more people and even entire people groups!

What initially would have appeared as a defeat on the surface was covertly revealed as a great triumph! In a time where one would have felt defeat, loss, and great hardship, and perhaps had thrown in the towel and given up, Leif, in this exact moment, remembered his history with the Lord and put on the ephod to seek his heavenly Father. What came out of those ashes was both unprecedented and historic and is continuing to bear fruit that will last for generations to come. This was a great trial that was turned into an unimaginable triumph because of abiding as a beloved son and heir to and through Jesus Christ.

Putting On The Ephod

> "In the waiting is the renewing, and in the renewing is the re-strengthening of the next steps." [1]
>
> — NICHOLAS BARTA

As we continue pressing into our abiding in Jesus, there will be times like that which papa Leif had shared where all seems lost. It is in these exact times that we must be just like Leif and remember to put on the ephod and go deep into God's presence to seek His council and the direction for prayer and actions that we are to take. Isaiah 40:31 teaches us,

> "But those who wait on the Lord Shall renew their strength; They shall mount up with wings like eagles, They shall run and not be weary, They shall walk and not faint" (Isa 40:31).

It is during times of uncertainty and discomfort that we are called to draw into the presence of God and wait upon the Lord for His direction and counsel. What seems impossible to do at that moment is the most practical thing to carry out, which is to call upon the Lord. The Prophet Isaiah wrote this through the inspiration of the Holy Spirit as an anthem for the Church of Jesus Christ to draw the strength of the Lord by waiting upon Him and being renewed in Him. That sounds like abiding to me! In the waiting is the renewing, and in the renewing is the re-strengthening of the next steps, therefore walking away from defeat or distress.

One of the most remarkable examples in the Bible of a hero remembering his history with the Lord and seeking Him amid distress and great suffering in order to be strengthened is king David. We read about this story in 1 Samuel 30, where David had returned with his men to Ziklag only to find it a heap of ashes. David and his men found that all of their wives, their sons, and their daughters were taken captive by the Amalekites, along with all of their supplies. The amount of anguish and grieving among the men was tremendous, so much so that David became distressed, for his own people spoke of stoning him. In this time of great distress, David called out to Abiathar so that he could inquire of the LORD what he should do. Can you imagine the distress of this situation?! When everything was lost, and all that they had built was burned to the ground with the greatest treasures of their family being taken from them, this man of God remembered the strength of abiding in the presence of the Lord and seeking the counsel of God.

When putting on the ephod, David was spiritually calling to remembrance his covenant with the Lord that included the preservation of the twelve tribes of Israel. In those days, the ephod had the twelve stones resembling the twelve tribes of Israel embedded into it. It was a holy garment that only the kings and priests would put upon themselves to minister to the Lord and seek His counsel. I find it significant that the symbolism of the ephod is of God's covenant with His chosen people, Israel. 1 Samuel 30:8 says,

> "So David inquired of the Lord, saying, "Shall I pursue this troop? Shall I overtake them?" And He answered him, "Pursue, for you shall surely overtake *them* and without fail recover *all*" (1 Sam 30:8).

In his great distress, when all those who were devoted to him turned on him, desiring to kill him, David did not react from fear of the unknown or panic at the uncertainty of the outcome. In the strength of his sonship unto God, David put on the ephod and inquired of the Lord, and the Lord spoke His word over the situation, and David attached his faith.

Later, in verses 18-19, we read the fulfillment of the prophetic word spoken by the Lord to David, that David had recovered all that was taken and that nothing was lacking, either small or great, sons or daughters or anything that was taken from them. David had recovered all. What seemed like a devastating defeat initially was then turned by the hand of God into a glorious victory, which included increased spoil from their enemies, the Amalekites. David not only recovered all that was lost, but by the hand of God, he also plundered the encampment of the enemy, took the spoil, and shared it with the elders across the land, which brought about a great unity within the nation under his future leadership as king over all of Israel.

Sons and daughters of God, this is exactly the heart of the Father for each one of us in whatever battles we may face in this life. Whatever spiritual battle you are facing, in Christ, you are assured of His triumph! Not only are we called to partner with God, to seek His heart, to put on the ephod and inquire of Him, but also to pray in accordance with what He shows us for the victory and not to stop short of the victory, but to plunder the encampment of the enemy!

In remembering that we are heirs of God and joint heirs with Jesus Christ, we can affirm that God is always faithful to His covenant and His covenant people. Our Lord God Almighty will always uphold His covenant with His chosen people, Jews, and Gentiles. As we abide in Jesus Christ, we are assured that, eventually, we will have the triumph of God. Even though we may lose some battles, the war is won by His triumphant Blood! We must recall our stones of remembrance when facing the giants in front of us so that we, through abiding in Jesus, can take new territory for the glory of the Lord!

Worship Music to Encounter Him [2]

11

VICTORIOUS SONSHIP
STONES OF REMEMBRANCE

Sometimes in life and in seasons of trial that I have faced, the Holy Spirit has beckoned me to call to remembrance past seasons of the faithfulness of God in and through my life. Written in my Bible and all over my home are memory stones of the Lord of past victories and prophetic words where the Lord brought His triumph and spoke to me significant things that were milestones in my walk with Him. These stones of remembrance can also be found all over the Bible. One of my favorite occurrences of when David used his memory stones with the Lord to face enemies in front of him is in the story of David versus Goliath.

1 Samuel 17 captures this incredible testimony of the Lord. In a time when the armies of Israel were paralyzed by fear and intimidation of their enemies, the Philistines, God had already spoken prophetically over Israel's future king His words of destiny that were answering prayers loud and clear! As we read this story, we learned that for 40 days, Goliath, the champion of the Philistine army, had taunted Israel, mocking the God of the armies of Israel. For 40 days, this giant intimidated and paralyzed the armies of God, going unanswered and unmet until God's anointed showed up.

When David had heard of it on the battlefield, he inquired what would be done for the one who would overcome this giant and deliver Israel from the oppression of the Philistine army. When king Saul had heard of David's courage to inquire about the reward, he called David to be brought to him. Saul had looked through his natural eyes at David and concluded initially that David would not overcome this giant Goliath. Now, let's pick up the story in verse 34 and see how David remembered his history with God.

> "But David said to Saul, 'Your servant used to keep his father's sheep, and when a lion or a bear came and took a lamb out of the flock, I went out after it and struck it, and delivered *the lamb* from its mouth; and when it arose against me, I caught it by its beard, and struck and killed it. Your servant has killed both lion and bear; and this uncircumcised Philistine will be like one of them, seeing he has defied the armies of the living God.' Moreover, David said, 'The Lord, who delivered me from the paw of the lion and from the paw of the bear, He will deliver me from the hand of this Philistine.' And Saul said to David, 'Go, and the Lord be with you!' So Saul clothed David with his armor, and he put a bronze helmet on his head; he also clothed him with a coat of mail. David fastened his sword to his armor and tried to walk, for he had not tested *them*. And David said to Saul, 'I cannot walk with these, for I have not tested *them*.' So David took them off. Then he took his staff in his hand; and he chose for himself five smooth stones from the brook, and put them in a shepherd's bag, in a pouch which he had, and his sling was in his hand. And he drew near to the Philistine' (1 Sam 17:34-40).

In this time of distress and impossibility, David remembered his history with the Lord and how the Lord was the one who brought victory when he faced the lion and the bear. David attributes the glory to the Lord for delivering him from the paw of the lion and the bear and prophecies forth the victory that the Lord will deliver him from the hand of this giant. Saul must have recognized the courage and the anointing of the Lord upon David and declared his blessing upon David to go and fight. Still looking at the situation through natural eyes, Saul clothed David in his armor and fastened his sword in David's hand. Knowing that David had never tested these, he took off man's attempt to bring about the victory of the Lord, and he walked in his anointing in God.

How often do we find ourselves in situations where we've done the same thing that David did by trying to figure out the situation and win through our own efforts and abilities apart from the Lord? This is the place where we must remember our covenant with the Lord just as David did and press into abiding in the Lord to seek the counsel of God for His strategy and to operate in His anointing to bring about victory. We read in verse 40 that David took his staff in his hand and that he picked five smooth stones from the brook to face his enemy.

The Lord spoke to me once that these stones were symbolic of David's memory stones with the Lord that were to be placed in his sling of victory to slay the spiritual giants and seize the land of promise. Our memory stones with God serve just like these smooth stones David chose, in that whatever battle we may face, we too each have a history with God where we can call to memory these stones of remembrance and load them in the sling of victory to slay the giants opposing us from walking in our promised land in the Lord. It only took one stone to take down this giant who was a man of war from his youth. So it is with the giants that we face in the spirit, that in Jesus Christ and through His triumph we too will be brought into victory as we take these weapons of our stones of remembrance in past victories we've won where God proved Himself faithful. The power of remembering our history with God when facing impossibilities in our present will produce new mindsets and greater faith that is needed to take down giants blocking us from entering our promised land and fulfilling our destiny in Christ.

As we remain abiding in Jesus, we are accessing the fullness of every spiritual blessing through our inheritance in Him made fully available to us through His Spirit in us. These very memory stones are like the stones on our ephod in the spirit where we call to remembrance how in the past God broke through our enemies and brought forth a testimony for His glory that is relevant and alive to the battles we face presently and in our future.

Like David, we must continually pull on our covenant with the Lord and seek Him in all things and in all ways as we continue abiding in Jesus.

The Battle Is The LORD's

In a prophetic proclamation, when facing his enemy, David spoke forth the word of the Lord, attributing the victory that was just moments away to the glory of the Lord by the hand of God. I love this so much because David had so much confidence in the Lord and his history with God that he knew with all of his heart that the Lord was going to bring a great victory for Israel. David spoke forth this prophetic decree in 1 Samuel 17:47, prophesying not only the victory he was about to experience, but by the Spirit of God, he prophesied about the victories we all would see in our lives by the hand of Almighty God.

> "Then all this assembly shall know that the LORD does not save with sword and spear; for the battle *is* the Lord's, and He will give you into our hands" (1 Sam 17:47).

This declaration is of utmost importance to each one of us today, no matter the battles we may face. We always remember that truly the battle is the Lord's and that our role as sons and daughters is to submit to God, resist the devil, and he indeed will flee from us (James 4:7). It is our God who fights for us, and we must remember to entrust the battles that we face unto the Lord and place it in His hands and not in our own hands. So often, and unknowingly, we clasp our hands around the situations and battles we face, trying to handle matters in the strength of our flesh rather than surrendering them into the hands of the Lord.

Part of the fruit of abiding is a life overflowing with trust in the Lord, that even when we are most capable or even when we are at our weakest, the victory will always and only come by the hand of the Lord, for the battle is the Lord's. Just as David shared with Saul his history with God and gave the Lord the glory for delivering him from the paw of the lion and of the bear, here we see the fruit of him pulling on those memory stones and remembering the strength of God that moved through him to grab the beard of the lion and overpower it. Such confidence in the Lord comes from abiding in Him and recalling with Him the times where He showed up and brought victories in the battles we've faced.

We are living in times where battles are intensifying, and the spiritual war at the end of days is at hand. God is searching all around for His sons and daughters upon the Earth who will place their full trust and confidence in Him alone, even when victory seems impossible. As His gaze captures our hearts, our only response can be to yield over everything afresh to His lordship and to entrust to Him the fullness of our confidence in His ability and not our own so that we can see the Lord bring about the victory and give Him all the glory.

"Worship-filled faith, combined with the prophetic word of the Lord that came from abiding with God, released the victory in a battle of assumed absolute defeat." [1]

— NICHOLAS BARTA

Worship is one of the strongest weapons of our warfare. Praise before a battle is won is the highest form of faith. I love the story in 2 Chronicles 20, where the armies of Judah were facing an insurmountable army with absolute certainty of their defeat. However, in this place, with multiple armies that had gathered together to take out God's covenant people, once again, we see the strength of God's people seeking the council of the Lord through fasting and prayer to receive direction and guidance from God. When you read this story, there is evidence of the power of remembering, putting on the ephod, and seeking the Lord with all one's heart in a time of great distress and fear.

King Jehoshaphat remembered Israel's history with the Lord and acknowledged their complete inability to defeat this insurmountable multitude. He ended with his faith declaration, "But our eyes *are* upon You" (2 Chr 20:12). What followed this corporate humility and time of prayer and fasting throughout the entire nation was God's response to sending the Holy Spirit and releasing the prophetic utterance through

Jahaziel. He spoke, "Thus says the Lord to you: 'Do not be afraid nor dismayed because of this great multitude, for the battle *is* not yours, but God's'" (2 Chr 20:15b). He further prophesied in verse 17,

> "You will not *need* to fight in this *battle*. Position yourselves, stand still and see the salvation of the Lord, who is with you, O Judah and Jerusalem!' Do not fear or be dismayed; tomorrow go out against them, for the Lord *is* with you" (2 Chr 20:17).

What happened in response to the word of the Lord was legendary. King Jehoshaphat and all the people responded in great faith with the word and worship unto the Lord as the king declared over the nation the wisdom and ordinance of God:

> "Hear me, O Judah and you inhabitants of Jerusalem: Believe in the Lord your God, and you shall be established; believe His prophets, and you shall prosper" (2 Chr 20:20).

Immediately, King Jehoshaphat consulted with the people and appointed the worshippers, who sang unto the Lord and went out before the army. As they worshiped, the Lord set ambushes against those who were against Judah, and they were utterly defeated. Worship-filled faith, combined with the prophetic word of the Lord that came from abiding with God, released the victory in a battle of assumed absolute defeat.

God is faithful to bring about His victory even in the most uncertain of situations and toughest battles. This is the place where we live fully surrendered, yet completely unconquered, by the impossibilities we face. As we turn and place our trust in the Lord, and entrust to Him the battle, He is at work in us. James 1:2-4 in the NIV says,

> "Consider it pure joy, my brothers and sisters, whenever you face trials of many kinds, because you know that the testing of your faith produces perseverance. Let perseverance finish its work so that you may be mature and complete, not lacking anything" (Jas 1:2-4 NIV).

In our trials, is the forging of our faith and the strengthening of our muscles of perseverance. In the process of abiding amid trials in hardship, our ability to yield to the Holy Spirit is of utmost importance. This is where He and only He can root up and pull out the rotten leavens that try to influence our souls. These leavens are the pain, disappointments, distresses, sorrows, grief, discouragement, and despair that we face in going through tense seasons and times of trial. Yielding to the Holy Spirit through sonship in abiding, will grant Him to impact our faith journey in the Lord. Submitting and surrendering to the Lord is the fullness of trust, and our ability to do so when we're living in the middle of the mystery of unanswered questions, is where He is strengthening us in sonship with the anointing of spiritual perseverance. We then become equipped for future battles to rise in His victory. Only the Lord truly knows what tomorrow holds, and perseverance with endurance is an anointing and grace that every person can benefit by growing in. The writer of Hebrews champions us in this growth of perseverance with endurance that is anchored in supernatural joy.

> "Therefore we also, since we are surrounded by so great a cloud of witnesses, let us lay aside every weight, and the sin which so easily ensnares us, and let us run with endurance the race that is set before us, looking unto Jesus, the author and finisher of *our* faith, who for the joy that was set before Him endured the cross, despising the shame, and has sat down at the right hand of the throne of God" (Heb 12:1-3).

There is no greater example of unrelenting perseverance with endurance flowing in supernatural joy than the example of Jesus Christ's journey through the cross. The supernatural grace that strengthened and enabled Jesus to endure the cross is the same grace made available to each of us through Him. This grace can only be accessed one way, and that is through abiding. Jesus abided in His Father continually and we see the strength of everything He did indeed flowed in and with and unto His heavenly Father.

> "Whatever overshadows you will shape you." [2]
>
> — LEIF HETLAND

What's incredible about this verse in Hebrews and the passage in John 15, is that the root word for 'endure' is the same as the root word for 'abide.' In Greek, the word for endurance is *hypomeneo* (Strong's G5278), which is derived from *hypo* (Strong's G5259), meaning "under," and *meno* (Strongs G3306), meaning "to abide." When we take the two root words formed together, it indicates that endurance is formed while abiding under. Now, isn't it incredible that the Lord formed languages together how He did?! The strength to endure and to persevere through resistance is found in abiding. As we surrender and submit the battle into the Lord's hands, we then open our hearts through abiding in the Lord, where He imparts His grace for endurance while we abide under the shadow of the Almighty (Ps 91:1). Whatever overshadows you will shape you, therefore as we abide under the shadow of the Almighty, we become overwhelmed by God and His incredible grace and not by our battles.

> "As you abide, you come alive." [3]
>
> — NICHOLAS BARTA

From this place, we can truly run our race with endurance, experiencing supernatural joy that is set before us. This enables us to abide under the shadow of Almighty God in the midst of the most trying circumstances and situations. As you abide, you come alive. God promises us in His Word that in doing so, we will indeed be filled with every spiritual blessing, and that is something that our hearts can shout with great thankfulness unto the Lord!

Thank-filled Hearts

One of my favorite stories that pulls in the significance of the power of remembering and recalling our memory stones with thankful hearts is the story of Joshua and the Israelites in Joshua 4. Joshua was a walking, living, breathing testimony of the power of God to grant supernatural endurance through abiding. Even though Joshua had to wait 40 long years to enter the promised land, God still gave him the strength of one who was half his age. When the time finally came to cross the Jordan and enter the promised land for the first time, one thing remained burning in Joshua's heart upon crossing, and that was to remember the Lord. Joshua was not simply thinking of remembering the Lord for his generation but desired to erect stones of remembrance that would be talked about for many generations to come. Upon giving direction to the twelve men from the twelve tribes of Israel regarding erecting the twelve memory stones in the midst of the Jordan, Joshua decreed forth,

> "that this may be a sign among you when your children ask in time to come, saying, 'What do these stones mean to you?' Then you shall answer them that the waters of the Jordan were cut off before the Ark of the Covenant of the Lord; when it crossed over the Jordan, the waters of the Jordan were cut off. And these stones shall be for a memorial to the children of Israel forever" (Josh 4:6-7).

This same question rings loudly for each of us today. What do these stones mean to you? What do the memory stones where God has come through and worked powerfully in your life truly mean to you for future battles you may face? Your history with God is one of the most valuable treasures you carry, for it is the strength of remembrance of all the times God has been faithful to bring about greater strength for the battles that lie ahead. Ensuring that we do not forget nor neglect to remember, not to grasp our hands around any impossibilities we face, but out of abiding to be strengthened with endurance and greater faith to entrust the battle to the Lord.

One of my favorite testimonies that serves as a memory stone forever embedded in my heart was during a time when my wife and I were facing significant spiritual warfare. Admittedly, the warfare was not enjoyable at all. However, pressing into the Lord during that season proved immensely fruitful for the seasons and trials that were ahead. During this season, the Lord spoke a powerful word of encouragement to me from His Word in 2 Samuel:

> "The Lord has broken through my enemies before me, like a breakthrough of water" (2 Sam 5:20).

As I meditated on this verse, my faith was strengthened in the midst of the spiritual hardship. The Lord was strengthening the muscle of perseverance in me to not only persevere through the resistance but to trust in Him to a new level through the pain and the unanswered questions. Although I had a long way to go to move beyond the discouragement and battle fatigue that I felt significantly in my heart, I took God at His Word.

I went on a bike ride sometime shortly after receiving that word to a lake by our house. As I ventured to the far east side of the lake, I saw a strange mist shooting up in the air that caught my attention and perked my sense of adventure. I rode over to the place to investigate what was causing the strange mist, and what I found astonished me. The dam that disperses water to other cities nearby was wide open for the first time in my viewing and was violently bursting water from its open valve. It was quite the sight! As I watched the water bursting forth with great power and splashing out onto the rocks 40-50 feet out, the Holy Spirit spoke to me. He said, "The Lord has broken through your enemies before you, like a breakthrough of water!" I was absolutely undone by the love and power of Father God. In His goodness, He planted that seed of His Word in my heart, then showed me an unforgettable demonstration of an example of that very word in the natural. This became permanently embedded in my mind as a memory stone of God's Word, His awesome power and His faithfulness to break through any enemy that opposes us to complete everything that He's called us to do for His glory. This led to an explosion of thankfulness for God's goodness and His intimate affection to have shown me He has heard our prayers and cry for His help.

Maybe you, too, have many stories of your own that you can recall and rise up in the present with increased thankfulness. With our hearts overflowing with gratitude for what the Lord has done, this weapon of thankfulness can be unleashed against any giants that stand in our path. A thankful heart is a merry heart, and this thankfulness is truly the fullness of praise as we believe in the Lord to bring supernatural victories in and through our lives for His glory! May your milestone memory stones be brought to remembrance at this time in your life so that increased thankfulness can overflow within your heart and strengthen you to rise in triumph, releasing the aroma of Jesus to all those around you. You will bear even greater fruit, and fruit that will remain.

12

BE FRUITFUL AND MULTIPLY

FRUITFULNESS IN ALL SEASONS

Although not everything that is true in the natural is true in the spirit, there are virtually countless ways the Lord teaches us spiritual principles through His natural realm. Be it known that although one cannot grow fruit in all seasons in some parts of the world, it is possible to remain fruitful in all seasons in the spirit. Just as God has created His divine order in nature with the four seasons, He also has created order for the seasons in the spirit.

Perhaps you have experienced what I am talking about here: in one season, you may have felt like things were springing forth and new life was happening as doors were opening to new opportunities. Can you remember the excitement and joy of the new growth that was happening? Or perhaps you have been in a season where things were being pruned, and what you'd known before was no longer fruitful for the season that was ahead. Just as we can view the distinct signs of the four seasons in the natural in most places of the world, so can we be discerning of the seasons that the Lord is taking us through in the spirit. Allow me to elaborate more.

Springtime in the spirit is a time when God is bringing new life, and new things are germinating, sprouting, and springing forth in your life and ministry. This is the season when God is watering the things He's planted within you so that new growth is coming forth to be a blessing in your life and the lives of those around you. The water of the Holy Spirit is most crucial, especially in the spring seasons in our lives, so that the new growth of the work God has done in our hearts is being nourished with the nutrients of Jesus in our lives. This is a time of excitement, joy, anticipation, and increased stewardship to tend to the new growth. Think of the farmer who tills the grounds and tends to his vineyards in the early spring so that the growth that is to come is stewarded well and that greater growth will be the result. It is a time of cleaning out the clutter in the landscape of our hearts and lives so that the grounds are ready for the Lord's planting.

In the summer, it is a season of flourishing from that which had been planted and is now growing and beginning to thrive. Summer is the season where green leaves are multiplying for the healing of nations. In this season, there is a great increase, and along with this multiplied growth comes pruning so that more fruit is produced. It is the season of the most sunlight, a time of receiving and releasing that which God is depositing. There is fresh air and liveliness in the atmosphere as things are built and established in this season so that in the season to come, there is the capability to collect the fruit that was labored for.

During autumn, the winds of change come, and it is a time of harvest. In fall, we collect, gather, and pull in plunder from our planting and tending labor in the spring and summer. In the seasons ahead, old dead things that will no longer be useful or fruitful are also being removed. This is the season of life in the spirit of sorting through the wheat and the chaff of our lives and through our ministries. This is the time of gathering the wheat into the barns, a great harvest for the Lord. It is an exciting time and yet also a messy time with God's beauty surrounding the changing of the seasons. New colors and new things that have not been seen before are shining with life in this season of change. As things are pulled in, preparation is happening for winter ahead.

In our modern-day Gregorian calendar, winter is the last season of the calendar year. This is the season of growing deeper roots, where there is tremendous growth in the unseen. This is the time of deeper intimacy being cultivated with the Lord and with loved ones. It is a time of resting and dreaming so that a new vision is cultivated for the future season. With this new vision, there is planning to prepare things needed in the season ahead. This is a special time of getting the heart of God to look forward to the new year while reflecting on all the fruits of breakthroughs and blessings that have come in the previous year. It is an exciting time to seek God's heart for what He wants in and through your life in the seasons ahead, while your roots are growing deeper in the soil of intimacy with Him. This is the time of invitation to dream with Him about your life and your call so that you would have His vision and eagle eyesight for the seasons that lie ahead.

Although each of these seasons is very distinct and noticeable, one thing remains true: in the spirit, you can experience parts of multiple seasons simultaneously. The Lord will take us through seasons in the spirit that may have elements of spring and fall or winter and summer and so on. The importance is to discern what season the Lord has you in and what His invitation is for you to steward in that season. As we discern correctly through the Holy Spirit what season He has drawn us into, we will then be able to correctly apply our efforts through abiding to align with His heart for us. When we are pressing into abiding with the Lord, fruitfulness will become the result.

Whether it is fruit of germinating, flourishing, harvesting or growing deeper roots, the importance of our heart aligning with the Lord will generate a greater output of fruit for His glory. God's heart in this abiding in Him, is that we thrive in all seasons of life. Even if there is 'harsh weather' in the spirit during our season, in abiding in the Lord, we will be strengthened through the heavy rains of spring, the heat and hail of summer, the winds of change and the removal of things in the fall and the bareness and bitter cold of the winter. It is through our abiding in Jesus that He fulfills His promise to us in 1 Peter in whatever season we are in with whatever spiritual weather or resistance we are facing.

> "After you have suffered for a little while, the God of all grace, who called you to His eternal glory in Christ, will Himself perfect, confirm, strengthen, and establish you" (1 Pet 5:10 NASB)

What has surprised me perhaps the most in the many years I've walked with the Lord is how valuable, yet sometimes unseen, is the great wealth of winter seasons. I have learned to cherish these root-growing seasons in the spirit where not much growth is seen visibly on the outside, but as I look back, I can see the great strength of spiritual roots that were established in what appeared to be a barren season. Here where I live, we have cold winters with lots of snow. There are no more leaves on the trees, yet what we lack, seeing above the surface of the ground, is much more than compensated by the tremendous growth below the surface. These winter seasons are when our trees grow great roots that are necessary to withstand strong winds and the challenging weather that lies ahead. If it weren't for these winter seasons, when the roots of trees grow deeper, there simply would not be strength to withstand the difficulties that lie ahead.

So this also rings true for us in this life, that winter is a crucial time in the spirit where we must grow deeper roots of intimacy and trust that become the foundations for greater oneness with the Lord lived through our life no matter what weather comes. These times shape you, not break you. This root growth is continual growth throughout our lives that will eliminate any propensity to bend towards becoming lukewarm or compromised in our faith walk. Deep roots mean a sound foundation. A sound foundation means a solid infrastructure of all that will be built upon it. I love the Scripture in Second Corinthians, where Paul teaches us about seeing from the unseen.

> "While we do not look at the things which are seen, but at the things which are not seen. For the things which are seen *are* temporary, but the things which are not seen *are* eternal" (2 Cor 4:18).

Our ability to see from the unseen will perpetuate greater hope, vision, and courage in seasons of trial. God is faithful to send His rain on the just and the unjust, and as we open our hearts in faith in Him, no matter what season we're in and no matter what difficulties we face, we then are truly pressing into abiding. As we abide closer, we then are accessing supernatural grace from God to carry us through into the new season and unfamiliar territory He's called us to. Cherish your roots, and you will yield the fruits.

You Are Called To Be Fruitful

For every born-again believer in Jesus Christ, there is a unique destiny and plan that God has for each one to fulfill. That plan, at the most basic truth, is that you would be fruitful. Living the lifestyle of abiding in the Lord will produce fruit, and that fruit is to remain. Jesus makes this truth clearly known as He spoke in John 15:16.

> "You did not choose Me, but I chose you and appointed you that you should go and bear fruit, and *that* your fruit should remain, that whatever you ask the Father in My name He may give you" (John 15:16).

Notice how Jesus did not put any pre-qualifiers on His statement of having appointed us and that the outcome would be fruit that remains. The whole context of what Jesus shares with us is built upon what He spoke in this chapter, which is about abiding. In abiding with Him through covenant, we are appointed by God and empowered by His Spirit to go about doing great work for the Lord that will generate and bear Kingdom fruit that will remain the tests of times and seasons. No matter where you've been in your life or where you currently are, be it you are fruitful, or you have felt like you've been wandering, in Christ, your journey is to be fruitful. God can even take the messiest and most broken of people and anoint them with His Spirit and His empowering grace flowing so that they become abundantly fruitful for His glory.

"If you stay close to God, He won't let you miss it." [1]

— MICHELLE BARTA

All over the Bible, we read of these men and women of God who were lost and broken, beaten and battered, yet God saw what He had placed in them from the beginning and called it to life through their yielding. If you stay close to God, He won't let you miss it. As you remain pursuant to continuing to yield your life daily over to the Lord and press into abiding intimately in Him, He is faithful to bring everything alive in you to become fruitful. Every gift, talent, and ability will receive the oil of anointing by the Lord as you abide in Him. Therefore, the output of fruitfulness from all that He has given you will exponentially increase as you continue oneness with Him.

You will be fruitful for the glory of God. It is your divine commissioning and command from the Lord from the beginning! After blessing them, God spoke His command to Adam and Eve in the garden,

> "Be fruitful and multiply; fill the earth and subdue it; have dominion over the fish of the sea, over the birds of the air, and over every living thing that moves on the earth" (Gen 1:28).

This was not an encouragement from the Lord, but a commandment from the Lord to His covenant people. Since God's Word can never return void, that very commandment extends to every one of us as His children here today and always (Isa 55:11). God has given to us as His people His holy ordinance to be fruitful and multiply for His glory upon the Earth and to take dominion over His creation. This is the very thing that Jesus came to restore back to humanity to be in the right relationship with Father God and to continue on being blessed by Him to fulfill His command of bearing fruit and multiplying it for His glory. Therefore, we read in Romans 8:19-22,

> "For the earnest expectation of the creation eagerly waits for the revealing of the sons of God. For the creation was subjected to futility, not willingly, but because of Him who subjected *it* in hope; because the creation itself also will be delivered from the bondage of corruption into the glorious liberty of the children of God. For we know that the whole creation groans and labors with birth pangs together until now" (Rom 8:19-22).

The glorious liberty of the children of God is to be restored to their original created order as God's agents of stewardship who exercise His rule and dominion over all of creation. We operate in the anointing of God to be fruitful for Him and to multiply that fruitfulness in this life everywhere He calls us to go and in everything He calls us to do. This tears down the darkness and the bondage of corruption that has oppressed creation, and it releases God's Kingdom in the power of the Holy Spirit through the finished work of Jesus, alive in us and moving through us!

What I love about this is that it is not simply reproducing something that has been done before, but partnering with the Holy Spirit in creative fruitfulness flowing from abiding. God has anointed and appointed you to be fruitful in the land He's called you to and to multiply His righteousness, holiness, healing, breakthrough, deliverance, and everything that He is to all those He calls you to. This is the Great Commission Jesus spoke of in Matthew 28 and combined with the revelation of fruitfulness and multiplication, we are exhorted to not only live fruitful but to live contagious for Jesus.

Freely we have received, so freely we shall give (Matt 10:8)! There is such a cost that other faithful servants of God have paid a high price for which we have freely received in the days we're living. Think of all the past and present heroes of the faith and the exploits they worked for the glory of the Lord to carry the Church to be where it is today. These ones paid a high cost by laying down their lives for us to freely receive the benefits of their obedience. Now it is our turn to pay a cost for future generations to receive as an inheritance that which we have invested through our obedience to God.

Think of all the Kingdom seeds that have been deposited in your life, perhaps even some that were deposited in you reading this book. The heart of the Father is that we would not merely be proficient in receiving these seeds and tending to them, but also be effective in multiplying these seeds even as we receive them. If you want a Kingdom seed to grow, give it away to someone else and sow it in their life right after you've received it. God will never be out given! As we move with the mindset from maintenance to multiplication, we will see explosive growth in discipleship as the seeds of God's Word sewn in our hearts are multiplied through our mouths and carried by the Holy Spirit into the hearts of others. Heaven is not a storehouse but a 'pour' house from which God is looking for faithful servants who will not squander the wealth of the revelation of His Word but will sow it faithfully into the lives of others to see Kingdom multiplication for God's glory. Give away right away and it will be multiplied in your sowing!

I long for the day to see the Church at large receive seeds of revelation from the Word after listening to a pastor's sermon on a Sunday morning, to then immediately go out to lunch afterward or to work on Monday and actively sow those seeds intently in the lives they encounter. Can you imagine and dream with me what it would be like if the Church at large were to take the fresh bread of revelation from a Sunday service, and have every son and daughter sow that seed of God's Word in multiple lives throughout the week? If just one person were reached and discipled through the Word every week by every person attending every church, the impact of those encountered in just one month's time would be beyond significant. The Lord is mobilizing His Church to move in a multiplicity mindset so that His Kingdom released in the Church would become His Kingdom released from the Church outside of the walls of the church buildings.

I believe this is the type of fruit Jesus was speaking of that would result from our abiding, and the multiplied fruit that Father God was speaking of back in the garden. God's exhortation in the Great Commission is for every believer to live fruitfully and to see people saved, healed, delivered, and set free through their very hands by the power of the Holy Spirit moving through them. Living with an intentional heart motive to pay the price so that the next generation can build upon what we've built will lead to a momentous move of the hand of God through the Church of Jesus Christ. Then, I believe collectively, the Church at large will work towards leaving a legacy as an inheritance for future generations for the glory of the Lord.

Living For Legacy

True fruitfulness, increased through generosity through the Church, will lead to exponential multiplication in the Kingdom. The heart of an anointed son or daughter of God living with a holy ambition to multiply seeds of the Kingdom continually in the lives of all he or she encounters draws like a magnet for the blessing of the Lord in their lives and through their ministry. Such intention to multiply fruitfulness will attract the favor of God and favor with man that will position such a person for even greater increase because of their faithfulness proven through their devoted actions. This is exactly what you read about in chapter five about the parable of the sower. This fruitfulness of a life marked by the evidence of multiplication will become set up by the Lord to leave a legacy that will continue to bear fruit that remains long after one transitions from this life into heaven.

For a man to leave a legacy is a good thing, but for him to leave a legacy for his grandchildren and beyond is a most wonderful thing. Proverbs 13:22 teaches us,

> "A good *man* leaves an inheritance to his children's children, But the wealth of the sinner is stored up for the righteous" (Prov 13:22).

In positioning our hearts to seek the will of the Father all throughout our life, and in our obedience to be obedient to all He calls us to, we are then being set up by God to produce fruit that will remain. Just imagine your life having such fruitfulness that it produces multiplication that leaves a legacy of inheritance for your children's children! Now, I'm certain that if I asked any believer, this question if they would desire this, without doubt, their answer would be yes. However, I believe the difference lies in one's willingness to endure suffering in hardship and to pay the price in this life so that such fruitfulness can be experienced in the lives of future generations. This is the invitation of the Lord to all of us who are alive today, and that is, can we burn with the revelation that the Lamb is worthy to receive the reward of His sufferings? We know that in this life, we will experience trials and hardship for Christ's sake, but as we have already read, the glory that shall be revealed in us cannot even be compared to these trials that we face (Rom 8:18).

Dream with me for a moment. What sacrifices and decisions can you make in your life now that could lead to a generational impact of great spiritual wealth released by God into the lives of those He's called you to influence? What would a compounding momentous multi-generational legacy of the Lord look like in a family of three generations or more?! I can only dream of the incredible wealth in the spirit of an unbroken chain of righteous momentum moving through a family line that is pure and wholly devoted to the Lord. A root system of righteousness across the generations in the family of God can leave a sustained and ever-increasing momentum of Kingdom change that will shape cultures in God's glory.

As we not only live yielded and set apart for the Lord in obedience to His will in the present but also have learned to honor wholeheartedly those who have gone before us, we will then combine the blessings of the Lord from the previous generation to the present generation which will lead to an explosion of Kingdom harvest. This type of movement of the Kingdom is a collective unity of the body of Christ, moving and working as one for the glory of Jesus Christ. In this, there is no room for selfish ambition, impure motives, greed for gain, or lusting for an increase of influence, but requires hearts completely sold out for God's will and God's way. This movement is truly a glorious manifestation of oneness by the power of the Holy Spirit.

As an illustration, consider God's creation of quaking aspen trees. The incredible fact about aspens is that they are the largest mass single organism in the world. On the surface, we see individual aspen tree groves, whereas many as thousands can be in a single grouping. The largest quaking aspen clone, called Pando, is found in the state of Utah, with about 47,000 trees spread over a hundred acres of land. Although we see these thousands of trees grouped together, we still only see the trees as individuals above the surface. But what we cannot see above the surface is that underground, these trees are one organism where their root system is one.

The incredible phenomenon through God's creation of aspen trees is that if there is a tree that is struggling to live, it will send out a signal through the root system to the surrounding trees nearby, who will then disperse excess nutrients through the root system to that struggling tree so that it can survive, regenerate, defend itself and thrive from the allocated resources of the surrounding community. These trees live, grow, and multiply as one since they share a single root system organism. What an incredible prophetic portrait of the Church of Jesus Christ learning and living abiding as one in Him!

Imagine God's Church learning to live and love abiding in the glory of oneness so that if there were any surrounding churches in the geographic territory that were struggling, then resources could be dispersed to help that church thrive. What could it look like for sons and daughters to be so captured by the Father's gaze, so in love with Jesus, and so engulfed in unity and oneness by the supernatural power of the Holy Spirit?! I believe it would look a lot like these aspen trees that stand strong in oneness in great numbers and, therefore, survive the harsh winds and droughts of the rough seasons over the years.

This is God's heart for His church to be unified with one heart and one mind by one Spirit so that a momentous legacy of glory can be passed down and increased through the ages to pull in the harvest of the ages leading up to Jesus' second coming. We are that harvest generation, and our mandate by God is to press so deeply into abiding in Him that we become just like Him to one another in the Body and shine for all the world to see. This is a great mystery of God's glory that can only be brought about by the Holy Spirit, and we must be hungry to pursue it with all our hearts.

Bound For Glory

According to Colossians, since as a believer you are in Christ and Christ is in you, there is an expectant hope for glory (Col 1:27). This very hope of glory is the very hope through which God has subjected all of creation for, and that is the hope of the glorious liberty of the children of God being made manifest by His Spirit into all of creation. These are the groans and labors with birth pangs that all the creation experiences until it will ultimately be delivered from its bondage and brought into glorious liberty through God's sons and daughters who know their true identity and take their authority over the works of darkness (Rom 8:20-22). This hope of the glorious liberty of the saints is what we are instructed to hope for and eagerly wait for with steadfast perseverance (Rom 8:25). Such hopeful and steadfast perseverance will generate a holy resoluteness to actively pursue the extension of God's Kingdom and the multiplication of seeds for His glory.

Since we are made in God's image and likeness, we are also formed in His glory to shine His glory for His glory. Every single son and daughter of God is bound for glory because of Christ alive in each one of us. This means that wherever we go and whatever we do, we carry the living answer of Jesus Christ to all the world. 2 Corinthians 3:17-18 says,

> "Now the Lord is the Spirit; and where the Spirit of the Lord *is*, there *is* liberty. But we all, with unveiled face, beholding as in a mirror the glory of the Lord, are being transformed into the same image from glory to glory, just as by the Spirit of the Lord" (2 Cor 3:17-18).

The glorious liberty that all of creation is longing for is manifested through the Holy Spirit of liberty alive inside you! Wherever the Spirit of the Lord is, there is the manifestation of liberty and freedom in Christ. Through us, the aroma of Christ is diffused and releases the fragrance of the knowledge of Him in every single place, leading to the fulfillment of Romans 8:21. We learn from this passage in 2 Corinthians that we all come with unveiled faces, meaning faces free of shame, condemnation, guilt, hiding and withholding who we truly are. Our unveiled faces are reflecting as in a mirror the very glory of the Lord to the world around us. In the glory of the Lord, we are being transformed into the exact fullness of the expression of Jesus in His image and likeness, and in the process of this transformation, God has ordained to be from a measure of glory to an increasing measure and revelation of His glory!

By the Holy Spirit of God, we are being transformed every day to be molded, shaped, and pruned to become just like Jesus. Jesus came to show us who His Father is and then gave us the blessing to make disciples over all the Earth by showing them who Jesus is. With the veil of shame and condemnation removed, we are presented by the Holy Spirit of God to the world as God's very own glorious children of light who bear His very image and likeness of love and oneness. Therefore, we are called by Jesus to let our light and glory of Him in us shine for all to see and experience the Lord of love and the God of all creation (Matt 5:13-16). Since we are called, blessed, anointed and sent by God, we then must embrace brave love and go out into all the world where God sends us to sow and release His glorious liberty into every people group, nation, tribe and sphere of influence that the Holy Spirit leads us into.

Hundredfold

There is perhaps nothing more valuable to God than His precious, glorious children from every nation, tribe, and tongue. Sometimes, at church gatherings or conferences, I am simply caught with amazement, with tears flowing at just the tiniest glimpse of the Father's wealth of every son and daughter of His. Although we cannot see the virtually endless depths of greatness and glory that He's deposited in each one of us, there are times where we see a glimpse of His glory manifested through a set apart son or daughter of His and it leaves us speechless. How could the tremendous great wealth of the Father ever be measured? How could we ever see the fullness of Him through His Body upon the Earth if it remains divided? Each and every son and daughter of God is blessed by Him to be a fruit bearer for His glory. The great beauty of this is that we truly need one another. We need the glory of Jesus in *you*.

We are marked by God to be transformed by Him from glory to ever-increasing levels of glory. That which is manifested through us will be the excellence of the power of God and not of us (2 Cor 4:7). For this is when the world will see the revelation of the glorious liberty of the children of God as the children of glory shine God's glory by the Holy Spirit for the lost to encounter the manifest love of God that leads to salvation in Jesus. Therefore, no matter what we face in this life, in Christ, we can rise in triumph, and we will not lose heart as we abide in oneness with Him and are strengthened by Him in all seasons and all situations. Paul wrote to the Corinthians:

> "*We are* hard-pressed on every side, yet not crushed; *we are* perplexed, but not in despair; persecuted, but not forsaken; struck down, but not destroyed—always carrying about in the body the dying of the Lord Jesus, that the life of Jesus also may be manifested in our body" (2 Cor 4:8-10).

In all situations and all seasons of life, we are encouraged by Paul through the Holy Spirit not to lose heart and to know that we carry the life of Jesus, who is working in us and through us to bring life to dry bones all around us. We are encouraged that even though we are being delivered to death for Jesus' sake, His life is being manifested in our mortal flesh. Day by day, we are indeed being renewed so that far greater glory can be made manifest through our surrendered lives as we abide in the true vine.

> "Therefore we do not lose heart. Even though our outward man is perishing, yet the inward *man* is being renewed day by day. For our light affliction, which is but for a moment, is working for us a far more exceeding *and* eternal weight of glory, while we do not look at the things which are seen, but at the things which are not seen. For the things which are seen are temporary, but the things which are not seen are eternal" (2 Cor 4:16-18).

Just as the strength of the root system of aspen trees is unseen, yet the evidence of their oneness is made known, so is the Church of Jesus Christ being strengthened in the unseen so that the manifestation of our unity in Jesus can be seen to bring about the harvest of the ages. God teaches us in His Word that it is through the very afflictions and challenges that we face that a far exceeding eternal weight of glory is at work within us. God's glory to work miracles in the unseen is eternal, and that very glory is at work in you. As you abide in Him and He in you, you truly have everything you need to be brought fully alive in your calling and destiny in this life. You will bring God's glory by the manifestation of His glory through your surrendered life found in the fruitfulness of abiding.

Go And Bear Fruit That Will Remain!

I champion you, sons and daughters in Jesus Christ, to go forth as contagious Christians and bear fruit in all seasons, from glory to glory. My prayer for you is that you would be a hundredfold fruit bearer for the glory of the Lord! That in every seed that is sown in you, you would multiply it a hundredfold for the Lord! I pray you would never lose heart and that you'd be strengthened with might in your inner man through the Holy Spirit in you, moving from one realm of God's glory to an ever-increasing revelation and manifestation of His glory in and through you.

I pray that whatever community you are in, you will find and experience the glory of Kingdom oneness within the Body of Christ in your region and nation. I bless you to increase day by day, season by season, in the glory of oneness with God through abiding in the Lord in the secret place. May you find joy unspeakable, hope abounding, and peace that surpasses all your understanding as you press further into abiding in the Lord. May the fruitfulness that comes from your abiding be ever-increasing and flowing throughout your whole life, and that through your obedience, others will find shelter, blessing, inheritance, and momentum as you continue to live unto the Lord.

I declare that the acorns of your faith would be planted and cultivated into a forest of righteousness, the planting of the Lord that He may be glorified! May you continue scattering seed into the wind of the Holy Spirit, who will carry the Kingdom revelation that's been deposited within you and multiply it into every area of influence and beyond that He's called you into. May you be found as a faithful servant unto the Lord who is fruitful in season and out of season so that your life would reflect the image, likeness, and love of King Jesus, leading multitudes to receive Him as their personal Lord and Savior.

I bless you, fruit bearer, to grow as you sow and to sow as you go, so that every seed you sow will be multiplied exponentially by the hand of God. May you be ever-increasingly blessed as you go forth and bear much fruit for the glory of King Jesus! Now go and bear more fruit and fruit that remains as you delight in abiding in and with the Lover of your soul being rooted in sonship unto Him.

"You did not choose Me, but I chose you and appointed you that you should go and bear fruit, and *that* your fruit should remain, that whatever you ask the Father in My name He may give you" (John 15:16).

ALL the glory, honor, and praise be unto the only One worthy; The Lamb of God and The Lion of Judah be glorified!

Worship Music to Encounter Him [2]

EPILOGUE

In reading this book, I hope that you have been enriched, encouraged, equipped and in ever-increasing, deepening love with Jesus. The lifestyle of abiding cannot be simply contained in a book or even in a thousand books. The aim here is to engage you to become nearer and more intimately connected to the heart of God, pressing ever so much closer to Him every day in your life. Your life is not merely intended to produce fruit. Your life should abide in Jesus and with Him in all that you do. Fruitfulness for His glory will be the natural byproduct of a life that flows in and reflects His glorious love. It is in pressing ever-increasingly deeper into the oneness with the Lord that Jesus spoke of in John 17 that we are becoming exponentially transformed into His glorious love to shine and reflect that same love for all those we encounter. Living abiding in the true vine positions us to live just like Jesus lived: in total dependence upon Father God through unbroken oneness with Him. This, too, should be our aim and pursuit in this life, for it is from this place that we will grow to become more and more like Jesus and live fruitfully and flourishing for His honor and glory.

I pray you will not merely have read this message, but that your life will become one marked by this message. I pray that God's glory would surround you and your family, bringing you from one measure of His glory to ever-increasing measures of His glory. I pray that your whole spirit, soul, and body will become wrapped up in the unfailing love of the Father through the lifestyle of love anchored in oneness that's flowing through abiding. Only then will it be said of your life that you are a person just like King David, a man or woman after God's own heart. Bless you, friend, as you endeavor to take this message of sonship and abiding and live it out in your life, family, workplaces, schools, and everywhere else the Father leads you. May your life be evidenced by a radical increase of the fruitfulness found in cultivating intimacy with God so that you live as a hundredfold seed spreader for the glory of God! Press on, never give up, and allow the soil of your heart to continually be tended by the Lord. Go and bear the great fruit of His love and that fruit that will remain!

ABOUT THE AUTHOR

Nicholas is a beloved son of the Father and a passionate, energetic, joyous lover of Jesus. He is a carrier and releaser of the joy of the Lord and the Father's Love. Nicholas burns with a vision of awakening, equipping, and empowering sons and daughters to find their true identity and sonship in Christ, with an increased revelation of the perfect, unfailing love of Father God. He encourages people to walk in a supernatural lifestyle that glorifies God. His heart is set on sons and daughters encountering the Father's love and discovering the unique greatness that God has placed within them, bringing about transformation around them. Nicholas believes there is such greatness and unlimited potential found in every person and that all are created in the image and likeness of God. Bringing people toward a deep revelation of their sonship in Christ fuels his heart with joy!

Nicholas' wife and best friend, Michelle, along with their three children, Joshua, Willow, and Aspen, spend their time outdoors enjoying God's creation through recreation and childlike playfulness. Nicholas achieved his Master of Arts in Leadership from Denver Seminary and is honored to serve the Lord with his wife as the lead pastors of a church they planted in Arvada, Colorado, called *Abba's Table*. They are the founders of *Soaring Sons & Daughters*. Together, they envision seeing the nations awaken to sonship, bringing about a move of the Spirit of Adoption to fall on generations who become set on fire for Jesus! They dream that such a move of the Spirit will send multitudes of sons and daughters soaring in the fullness of their purpose and destinies in the Lord.

With a heart that burns for the nations to know the love of the Father and for all to discover their sonship in Jesus Christ, Nicholas loves traveling itinerantly to speaking engagements wherever God calls him to! As more children of God discover their place as a family at the Father's table and confidently live in sonship immersed in the Father's love, remarkable growth in the Kingdom Family movement of God will occur. This unity of family will bring about incredible transformation to the world with God's powerful love!

Nicholas Barta

Lead Pastor, Author, and Speaker

ALSO BY NICHOLAS BARTA

SOARING IN SONSHIP SERIES 3-BOOK SET

The ***Soaring In Sonship Series*** will draw you into an invitation to encounter the Father's love for you as you discover yourself fully in Him. Enjoy the journey and set sail on an endless ocean of God's perfect love for you. May you uncover the immeasurable greatness God placed within you as you pursue fulfilling your calling in Him!

Available on Amazon

DISCOVERING SONSHIP:
UNCOVERING THE GREATNESS WITHIN

BOOK 1

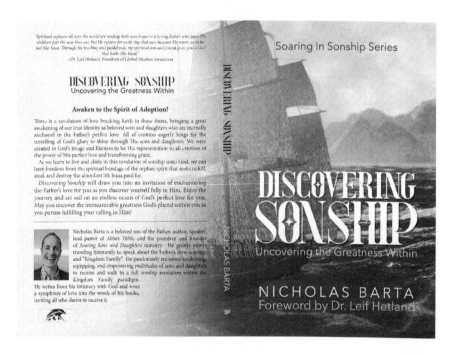

In *Discovering Sonship: Uncovering the Greatness Within*, learn about the revolution of love breaking forth in these times, bringing a great awakening of our true identity as beloved sons and daughters who are eternally anchored in the Father's perfect love. All of creation eagerly longs for the unveiling of God's glory to shine through His sons and daughters. As we learn to live and abide in this revelation of sonship unto God, we can have freedom from the spiritual bondage of the orphan spirit that seeks to kill, steal, and destroy the abundant life Jesus paid for. [1]

Available on Amazon

SOARING EAGLES ACADEMY eCOURSES

"Father Loves You" eCourse - Register Today!

Hungry for deeper intimacy with the Father's love? Join the *Father Loves You eCourse* to encounter His love and gain tools for deeper connection. Become a river of transformative love and live as a Love Agent of God, bringing the Father's love into every sphere. Say YES to this journey of living fully loved and drawing others to Jesus in you, the hope of glory!

SOARING EAGLES ACADEMY E-COURSES

https://soaringsonsanddaughters.com/register/father-loves-you-ecourse/

DISCOVER SOARING EAGLES ACADEMY

Soar Higher & Awaken to Your Destiny

Now is the time to awaken to your destiny and dive into God's presence. Experience His love and uncover the gifts He placed within you to fully occupy your spiritual territory. You carry unique greatness for God's glory, and all creation eagerly awaits the revealing of God's glorious children. Invest in encountering His love, become equipped and empowered, and soar like never before! [3]

SOARING EAGLES ACADEMY WEBSITE

https://soaringsonsanddaughters.com/soaringeaglesacademy/ [4]

RESOURCES

For more information, books, and the latest updates, please visit:
SoaringSonsandDaughters.com
9975 Wadsworth Pkwy., K-2 #267
Westminster, CO 80021

NOTES

Copyright

1. Soaring Sons and Daughters Website, http://soaringsonsanddaughters.com/

1. Living In Life-Union with Jesus

1. Quote, "Your giving should always flow out of your growing as you receive today your daily bread of Jesus."~Nicholas Barta
2. Quote, "Abide in the overflow." ~Nicholas Barta
3. *Abide Acoustic- Dwell Songs*, Aaron Williams, https://youtu.be/hXKbc7Ycaf8?si=TvCMAe3_-JoJvoNA

2. The Gentle Heart Gardener

1. Quote, "Prayer paves the road of the access points to the deepest parts of us and intimately connects them to the fullness of all of Him." ~Nicholas Barta
2. Quote, "Leave the striving and return to abiding! ~Nicholas Barta
3. Quote, "This means that the river of life flows where you *abide*." ~Nicholas Barta
4. *Tend*, Emmy Rose, Bethel Music, https://youtu.be/HSB4poSt7UE?si=fVPJ6j6AhTZoocXF

3. A Renewed Mind

1. Stronghold Chart
2. Quote, "Pruning yields better mental processing." ~Nicholas Barta

4. Abiding Rest

1. Quote, "Be *with* Him rather than trying to get *from* Him." ~Nicholas Barta
2. Quote, "To be *at* rest, we must live *in* rest with Him."~Nicholas Barta
3. Quote, "His yoke is LOVE." ~Nicholas Barta
4. Quote, "You are at your best when you're living in His rest." ~Nicholas Barta
5. Quote, "In the stillness, true strength is found." ~Nicholas Barta
6. *Come Away*, Bryan McCleery, https://youtu.be/QFdDV_uUpAA?si=4qaHCgWIikC1XCb4

5. The Parable of Parables

1. Quote, "In the stillness, true strength is found." ~Nicholas Barta

6. The Fear Of The LORD

1. Quote, "The holy fear of the Lord alive in one's life will never be void of pure, raw obedience to God." ~John Bevere
2. Quote, "Sometimes fruitfulness has to grow in one season before it's seen in the next." ~Nicholas Barta
3. Quote, "Kingdom alignment will always precede Kingdom assignment." ~Leif Hetland

7. Obedient Love

1. Quote, "Our humility before Him is to acknowledge our weaknesses and inability to produce or do anything apart from Him." ~Nicholas Barta
2. Quote, "Full dependence that God will lead you, opens you to see the path He's called you to follow." ~Nicholas Barta
3. Quote, "In the process of the pressing is where the oil is formed." ~Nicholas Barta
4. *River of Love*, Cageless Birds, Joel Case, https://youtu.be/WS2xH2VzyRk?si=hBcBkPO1G2jt1TWs

8. A Friend Of God

1. Quote, "There isn't a closer, more intimate invitation than oneness." ~Nicholas Barta
2. Quote, "We must lay it all down before we pick anything up." ~Nicholas Barta
3. Quote, "Pray for the grace of humility." ~Nicholas Barta
4. Quote, "Humility is the key to accessing increase." ~Nicholas Barta
5. Quote, "As we remain in life union with Jesus, the supernatural becomes our natural." ~Nicholas Barta

9. Abiding Prayer

1. Quote, "Assumption can be an enemy to abiding prayer because it's rooted in the flesh and is reliant upon our ability apart from God." ~Nicholas Barta

10. Trials Into Triumphs

1. Quote, "In the waiting is the renewing, and in the renewing is the re-strengthening of the next steps." ~Nicholas Barta
2. *Know (Be Still)*, Jeremy Riddle, https://youtu.be/A8TtOIMaKKA?si=wjccCjXE9u4lYawu

Notes

11. Victorious Sonship

1. Quote, "Worship-filled faith, combined with the prophetic word of the Lord that came from abiding with God, released the victory in a battle of assumed absolute defeat." ~Nicholas Barta
2. Quote, "Whatever overshadows you will shape you." ~Leif Hetland
3. Quote, "As you abide, you come alive." ~Nicholas Barta

12. Be Fruitful And Multiply

1. Quote, "If you stay close to God, He won't let you miss it." ~Michelle Barta
2. *Full Attention*, Jeremy Riddle, https://youtu.be/eCtu9eKgMYM?si=f0L_e9CS7-qDkA-1

Also by Nicholas Barta

1. *Discovering Sonship: Uncovering the Greatness Within,* My Book
2. Soaring Eagles Academy E-Courses, https://soaringsonsanddaughters.com/register/father-loves-you-ecourse/
3. Soaring Eagles Academy Video, https://vimeo.com/936790818/f08fdf5e08
4. Soaring Eagles Academy Website, https://soaringsonsanddaughters.com/soaringeaglesacademy/

Made in the USA
Columbia, SC
02 February 2025